CONRAN'S
STYLISH INTERIORS

CONRAN'S
STYLISH
INTERIORS

ELIZABETH WILHIDE AND ANDREA SPENCER

With photographs by Simon Brown

Introduction by Terence Conran

Little, Brown and Company
Boston • Toronto

FIRST U.S. EDITION

LIBRARY OF CONGRESS CATALOGUE CARD NO. 86–50481

First published in 1986 in the United Kingdom by Conran Octopus Limited.

Conceived, designed and produced by
Conran Octopus Limited

Printed and bound in Great Britain by
William Clowes Limited, Beccles and London

CONTENTS

INTRODUCTION

Style is not only hard to define, it's also one of the most overworked words in the dictionary. Yet it's still the best way to describe the rare ability to be appropriate and original – the flair that the best interiors always display.

It used to cost a good deal of money to decorate and furnish a home with style, since this invariably involved the expensive services of specialist suppliers and skilled craftsmen. While high-quality materials and workmanship have not suddenly become cheaper, today it is possible to achieve an equivalent result without spending a fortune. Increasingly, well-designed and well-made fittings, fabrics and furniture are available at prices everyone can afford. This is in no small way due to advances in technology and manufacturing which mean that everything from paints to door handles, and from floor coverings to light fittings, is offered in greater variety and to better standards than ever before. With the enormous range of good-quality home products on the market, the customer benefits from a breadth of choice that would have been hard to imagine only a few decades ago.

Books and magazines today contain a wealth of information on decorating techniques, which means that anyone can be privy to the trade secrets of the professionals and the solutions of resourceful individuals. Doing-it-yourself need no longer imply an approach that is as short on style as it is on funds but has become a satisfying outlet for creative ideas. And in these conservationist times, dedicated to restoring and recycling the past, everything from antique bathroom fixtures to period fireplaces can be found in junk shops, markets and architectural salvage companies. Altogether this amounts to a great resource for the home designer with an eye for economy and a taste for style.

The homes featured in this book clearly show that what constitutes style will always be open to wide interpretation – even debate. Nevertheless, despite the variety displayed here, there is a surprising consistency when it comes to basic approaches.

In all of these examples, considerable effort has gone into research and planning: problem areas have been identified and practical requirements taken into account, while the full

The ultimate minimal home
of architect John Pawson and
Hester van Royen.

Angela Hewitt in the hallway
of her London apartment.

INTRODUCTION

Writer and designer Maureen Walker at home.

A subtle mural in the apartment of Roger Britnell.

range of decorative possibilities has been thoroughly explored, whether this involves choosing a bedcover or deciding on a kitchen layout. These investigations have often led to unusual sources for materials or furnishings – in many of these homes you will find flea market discoveries happily co-existing with store purchases. This highlights an important aspect of planning: working to budget. Deciding how you spend your money involves ensuring that enough is allocated to the important ingredients. But equally important, where money is spent it must be spent where it will be most effective – for example, in one home this was a good floor to unify the space and in another a fine modern table which is the focus of interest in a minimal room. In every case, where funds are limited, this has acted not as a constraint but as a stimulus to the imagination.

Colours and themes are always consistent throughout a house or apartment, but this crucial part of design is often misunderstood. This does not mean a lifeless co-ordination, using, say, the same pattern for wallpaper, bedlinen and upholstery and finding you are sick of it after a week. It means a subtle combination of tones, textures and patterns, and a wholehearted approach, not a jumble of styles.

Attention has also been paid to detail, whether this consists of a wall finish or an electric socket. It cannot be stressed enough that it's the details that make or break a room: 'God is in the details' could not be more true. You can put enormous effort into decorating and furnishing a living room and ruin the effect with trailing wires or bad lighting, the wrong rug or a prominent and ugly television. Some corners *can* be cut, and this book is full of helpful suggestions for saving time as well as money, but do not underestimate the importance of details. Choose your wastepaper bins with the same dedication and eye for colour, shape and impact as you would a painting or a large piece of furniture.

'Less is more' is another good guideline. Knowing when to stop is important – what you leave out can be just as effective as what you put in.

The final element which goes to make a home stylish is not to do with strategy or method at all. The interiors in this book are often unorthodox, sometimes ingenious, but always full of personality. You get a definite sense of the people who created them. I am sure that not one of them could care what you or I think of their taste but, although I like some more than others, I respect them all. A confidence shines through in every example – the confidence the people have in their own ideas and the fact that they are not afraid of expressing those ideas in their own homes. That is the secret of style and the reason it is not dependent on money. I can think of many examples of interiors where unlimited funds have resulted in unmitigated dullness. Equally, some of the most stylish and original homes I have visited have been decorated on a shoestring.

This book includes a few interiors where larger sums of money have been spent. or where the owners have inherited beautiful objects, even the homes themselves, but in every case there is a solution or an approach which will help you if you are working to a small budget. These strategies will help you devise a style of your own, whether you are short of money or time, or both.

Marie Chaumette and Patrick Poirier's apartment in Paris.

A fine kitchen view in the Long Island beach house of Bob and Joan Bayley.

9

PERIOD FEATURES

Buying a period property is fraught with pitfalls. Spotting potential beneath the inevitable neglect demands imagination; distinguishing between structural and superficial decay requires an expert's eye. If you make the wrong decision, the process of restoration can wind up being expensive and time-consuming – but if you make the right one, you get much more than you pay for.

Part of a late Georgian terrace development dating from 1830, this apartment has been empty for ten years and badly maintained for much longer. The hall was cluttered up with a builit-in kitchenette; the bathroom was 'gruesome'. Layers of dark varnish covered the parquet floors and the fireplaces were either blocked up or obscured with paint. Since there was also no heating or modern servicing the purchase price was low. The scale of the problem might have put off anyone without limitless supplies of time and money, but hard work, ingenuity and good planning have made a transformation that is attractive and economical.

Beneath the dereliction, the structure was sound and most of the original features were intact. Apart from fine oak and teak parquet floors, these included ceramic tiling, original windows, fireplaces and mouldings. Equally important, the generous proportions of the rooms had not been spoiled by conversion and few structural changes were necessary.

To save money, Jerry and Angela Hewitt, the new owners, carried out the bulk of the work themselves – moving in to tackle the floors with an industrial sander even before contracts were exchanged. The next step was to replan the bathroom. Working out how to accommodate a 1.8m (6ft) bath, Jerry, an architect, came up with the happy solution of the obelisk, which protrudes into the hall introducing an appropriate neo-classical note. Angela, head of a London fashion school and an accessory designer, restored the tiled hall floor, scouring it with acid, and spent several days clearing paint from the living room fireplace.

The decoration is simple and sensitive, taking care not to overwhelm the Georgian detailing. The temptation slavishly to reproduce the past has been resisted, creating a harmonious interior that nevertheless captures the spirit of its period.

1 The entrance hall presents a cool vista culminating in the obelisk construction. On either side of the arch, plaster barleytwist columns were added. Lights are inset in the capitals. Surrounded by an ornate Victorian frame, the mirror is actually in two sections and hides a cupboard. Heavy-duty glue was used to stick the sheet mirror to the doors, which press shut.

2

2 In the bathroom, clever planning accommodates a 1.8m (6ft) bath with a shower fitting in an obelisk-shaped alcove.

The stonework effect on the wall was quickly and cheaply achieved by papering with two tones of marbled writing paper. The sheets were stuck in place with wallpaper paste and then covered with many coats of polyurethane varnish to protect the surface.

3

3 The kitchen/dining room was relocated in one of the two grand reception rooms and designed to live up to its elegant setting. The first task was to clear the disfiguring dark varnish from the oak parquet floor. Using an industrial sander, Angela went over the surface gently but consistently, evening it up. She then applied coats of yacht varnish, which is cheaper than standard varieties because it comes in such large sizes, and also dries to a deeper shine.

Taking the place of kitchen units, an Edwardian pedestal sideboard bought at an auction was converted to take a gas hob or stove top, an adaptation made by cutting through the solid 50mm (2in) top with a jigsaw. A dishwasher was slotted in underneath and the cupboards, fitted with the original butler's trays lined with green baize, house cutlery and crockery.

The rest of the cupboards and worksurfaces were decorated by Angela to give them a more refined appearance. The cupboard panels and the worktop were both marbled, using emulsion tinted with water-based stainers. Veining in white and grey was painted in freehand and then softened in the traditional way with a pheasant feather. Dabbing the surface with a sponge helped to simulate the cloudiness of the real material. Marble slip tiles make a neat edging along the back of the units.

The space is dominated by a large bow window looking out over an internal light well. As a decorative touch, stars cut out of gold wrapping paper were stuck to the ceiling.

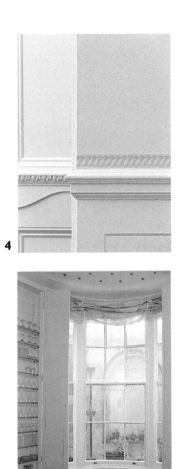

Draping a large, curved window can be an expensive and intricate business. Curtains would require yards of material and a complicated heading. Here the problem is neatly solved by making a simple Roman blind from a cheap fabric – Indian cotton voile shot with lurex, so light that it draws up easily. To fit the blind around the curve of the window, it is attached with Velcro, which also makes cleaning easier.

4 The understated decoration in clear, pale colours is one of the most important aspects of this scheme. To match the decoration on the kitchen cupboards, panels were painted onto the walls below the chair rail, their shapes created by masking out with tape. A fine shaded grey outline simulates the raised edge of a moulding; inside this border, emulsion paint tinted with artists' stains was used for the marbling.

5 The shutter housings on either side of the bow windows were empty and, rather than nail the panels shut, Angela decided to make use of the space for cupboards. Glass, 6mm (¼in) thick, was used for shelving. Since the walls are not true, careful measurements had to be taken and a separate pattern, or template, made for each shelf before it could be cut. They are held in place with brass library shelf fixings.

6 An original fireplace, on the other side of the kitchen, has been lovingly restored and painted in plain white to display the fine modelling. Plaster reproduction capitals mounted on the walls make dramatic uplighters. A butler's tray discovered in an antique market carries a selection of drinks. At night, with the glow of candlelight, the room becomes a formal setting for dinner parties.

13

Modern radiators always look out of place in period rooms. Disguise is one solution; an alternative is to install older models, which strike a less discordant note (see 2).

8

7 The living room, beautifully proportioned with its fine plasterwork mouldings and expanse of window, has more than repaid all the effort spent in restoration. As in the kitchen, the first job was to sand and varnish the floor.

The rich-looking grey taffeta blind was an extremely cheap solution for covering such a large area. The fabric came from a theatrical suppliers and cost much less than a department store equivalent.

Standard furniture would simply disappear in a space of this size, so money was spent having the extra-long sofas made to order. The upholstery, however, was cheap – Indian cotton bought wholesale and dyed. Scattered over the sofas are one of Angela's most delightful discoveries: World War II escape maps, printed on silk in fantastic detail and made up into cushion covers.

8 Torch lights from a junk shop flank a lithograph by Tim Mara opposite the living room fireplace. The sofa table was a present, renovated by rubbing with wire wool and polishing with beeswax.

Topiary trees, reminiscent of eighteenth-century formal gardens, were made by Angela's mother, who constructed them by covering wire frames with dried flowers and plants.

15

COLOUR MAGIC

Colour is cheap. It's the simplest way to brighten up a dull room, make a chilly one warm or create mood and atmosphere. But there is an art to using it.

When Nicola Gresswell came to decorate her home, it was her work as an artist that provided both the problem and its solution. She chose the house, a nineteenth-century terrace, because it faces northeast, giving a cool, even light which is ideal for a studio but chilly and uncompromising to live with. The answer was to apply her own skills to warm up the interiors with a vibrancy of colour. The success of the result is due not only to a fundamental understanding of how colour works but also a gift for composition.

To get the most from paint you have to move away from the standard ranges and be willing to experiment. Nicola tried out many different shades and techniques on sheets of hardboard before committing herself to a final choice. Throughout the house, all the walls were primed with three coats of 'pastel base' eggshell, a white paint that has no pigment added. This gives a soft, lustrous finish which provides the ideal ground for a 'scumble' glaze. The glaze is a transparent, oil-based paint, which when tinted with artists' oil colours can be used to create a variety of finishes. Nicola applied the scumble glaze to the eggshell base using a range of techniques – sponging, stippling and ragging. Each colour and technique was finally adopted after endless experiments. A final coat of varnish protected the surfaces.

Paint is only part of the story. Nicola waited three years before she found the right red sofa for her living room and admits to spending a large part of her budget on the living room carpet because the cool blue perfectly complemented the yellow walls. But much of the inspiration came from things she already owned, collected over the years as subject matter for her paintings: fabrics, china, ornaments, children's toys, and flowers – real and fake. They range from the tasteful to the frankly kitsch.

Behind the freshness and spontaneity lies a great deal of deliberation, with each room composed like an intimate still life. As if to underline the point, Nicola's paintings depict many of the objects on show about the house. You have to look twice to see where art meets life.

1 Three primary colours, in a bold but considered gesture, make a warm welcome in the living room. A faint red ochre glaze scumbled over the top with a fine natural sponge and stippling brush adds warmth to the yellow walls. Scandinavian self-assembly chairs and a bright red trolley make a focal point in the bay. The blue and white ceramic pots are Chinese garden seats from London's Chinatown, used as stools or small tables.

2 A painting of strawberries, by Nicola, is hung over the piano, its frame dragged in acrylic paint. Favourite ornaments and a vivid scarf set off the dark wood; a painting by Elizabeth Taggart is propped on the music stand.

3 Chinese horses march along the recess of a 1920s' fireplace. The grate was found in the house and restored. The horses are a childhood collection.

4

5

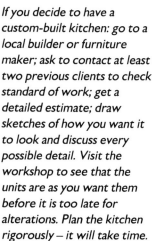

If you decide to have a custom-built kitchen: go to a local builder or furniture maker; ask to contact at least two previous clients to check standard of work; get a detailed estimate; draw sketches of how you want it to look and discuss every possible detail. Visit the workshop to see that the units are as you want them before it is too late for alterations. Plan the kitchen rigorously – it will take time.

4 To design your own kitchen and have it made to your specification, rather than to buy ready-made units, can be cheaper and more practical. Every detail of this room was planned to suit Nicola's particular requirements. Two cupboard doors fixed together open vertically to make an air extractor. Nicola specified the layout so that all items are instantly accessible and food preparation and cooking are

carried out with practical ease. Banks of power points provide countertop flexibility. A decor panel hides the refrigerator; all the cupboard door panels were painted with eggshell, which doesn't show marks. Rubber washers behind the china knobs on the cupboards cushion the impact.

A frieze of blue and white Dutch tiles adds cheerful decoration, along with the row of china jugs displayed on the top of the cupboards.

5 The dining area brings a hint of the living room colour scheme to the kitchen. The kitchen is linked to the living room by large double doors, with the dining table standing to one side of the room. The cool blue linoleum floor helps make the through view coherent. One cupboard was designed to store exactly six of the folding red chairs.

6

6 The studio serves as a plain background for work and display. It was formerly a first-floor drawing room and runs across the entire width of the house. Large windows provide excellent natural light for Nicola's work. The walls were painted with pastel base and the ceiling a slightly darker shade of off-white. Stripped, sanded and varnished, the wooden floor makes a warm, practical surface.

Unusual toys, china and teapots are all treasured and colourful objects that have a tendency to turn up in two dimensions in Nicola's paintings. Here they are displayed on shelves that line both alcoves on either side of the fireplace. All the woodwork and shelving in the studio was painted in a mixture of eggshell and gloss (60 : 40), which gives a lustrous, but not overly shiny finish. The shelves are all movable; an ogee beading, available off the peg from timber merchants or DIY shops, makes a neat detail at the top.

Further storage for finished paintings and materials is provided by the plan chest, acquired cheaply at a government surplus sale. The windows are covered with lilac pleatex blinds, which draw up neatly into the recesses by day. Plants flourish in the good light, adding a homey touch to the studio.

When your home is also your place of work, deciding which room to devote to a studio or office can be a problem. If you settle for a corner of a living area or a tiny spare room, your work will suffer. A big, airy room such as this studio not only creates a productive atmosphere, but can be kept separate from the activities of the rest of the household.

19

7 Halfway up the stairs, a corner of the landing offers the chance for more display. A marble-topped semi-circular hall table, one of the original features found in the house when Nicola moved in, here provides a setting for orchids, cyclamen and begonia. The neutral walls of the hallway not only make a good exhibition space for paintings, but also help separate one colour scheme from the next.

8 The main bedroom decor makes use of strong colours to generate a sense of intimacy. Primed with white eggshell, the walls were painted with cerulean blue glaze. A stippling brush removed traces of brushmarks and the glaze was then ragged off using a bunched cloth. A contrasting soft pink was stippled on the ceiling. Plain curtains and carpet, and a seersucker duvet cover, accentuate the feeling of cosiness

Ragging, the paint technique used here on the walls, creates an insistent, dense finish. Because the texture is so obvious, it is important to keep the rest of the decoration as plain as possible to prevent the overall effect becoming too busy. The print you can achieve with a rag depends on what kind of cloth you use, but in general tends to be rather defined, so it is best to stick to soft shades to avoid a brash look.

By contrast, stippling, the technique used for the ceiling, is a gentler finish. It is achieved by lifting off patches of wet glaze with the squared end of a stippling brush, creating a lightly textured, dappled look. Stippling can be an extremely tiring technique, especially if you are tackling a large area.

9

10

9 The guest room has a 'pink' theme. The vibrant walls were designed to complement the pale aquamarine carpet, a colour picked up in the dragged frame of the painting.

Marbling is especially effective on appropriate surfaces such as fireplaces. The plain stone fireplace in the guest room was first painted with off-white eggshell and then sanded down before being marbled in shades of matt grey oil-based paint.

A squirrel brush was used to draw the 'veining'; a sponge soaked with turpentine blurred the lines to give a realistic effect.

Plastic tulips make a vivid and witty contrast to the grate. The hearthrug is a 1920s' New England hooked rug, a treasure Nicola found in her grandmother's house.

10 A length of Japanese silk is pinned over the window to cover the blind, which is set into the recess.

The cupboards were specially designed by Nicola; note the practical shelving system for clothes' storage.

Unusual carpet colours often turn up at affordable prices at sale time – this one was a remnant found in a sale. The alternative, having carpet specially dyed, can be prohibitively expensive.

Marbling requires a certain degree of skill. It's best to practise copying a piece of real marble beforehand. The aim is not to produce a realistic representation of the original but an effective stylization. The essential characteristics you should try to suggest are cloudiness, veining and smoothness of finish.

21

SPLIT LEVEL

Apartments present few opportunities for increasing floor area because extensions are usually ruled out. But in older, high-ceilinged properties, making a gallery is a good way of creating extra space – and if a room is really lofty it can even be divided in two by building a new floor halfway up the walls. Both of these solutions, together with other well-considered structural changes, have been adopted here.

The owner, Linda Sparks, a 'frustrated interior designer', bought this apartment because of its period details, high-ceilinged living room and adjoining conservatory. But there were drawbacks. Because the floor area was quite small, the living room looked out of proportion. The bathroom was tiny; the kitchen was located in a long, narrow room down a spiral staircase. Storage was minimal. To improve the use of space and help her plan a gallery, the owner consulted Carl Falck, a friend who is an architect. His scheme provided two new rooms, doubled the bathroom area and allowed access to a roof terrace – altogether incorporating five different changes in level.

The gallery, designed to accommodate a bedroom, also helps to correct the proportions of the living room. An attic was discovered over the bathroom; knocking through into this area from the living room created space for the gallery and enabled the bathroom itself to be enlarged. Since the original kitchen had such a high ceiling, the floor could be raised halfway up the walls, with the new kitchen relocated in the top half and the lower portion used as a storage room for clothes and cleaning equipment. An archway and a short flight of steps lined with plants now connect the new kitchen and the conservatory, with double doors opening out onto a roof terrace. Access to the terrace effectively doubles the area of the apartment in fine weather.

To save money, the architect was brought in only for the design stage; getting the job done was another story. When the owner discovered that the builders had taken down a load-bearing wall without propping up the structure she hurriedly moved into the gutted apartment, camping out on the floor to avert further disasters. All ended well, but the experience taught Linda the value of detailed estimates and specifications, and the importance of constant supervision.

1 In the living room
emphasis is on subtle contrasts of tone and texture. The marble coffee table, black plastic sideboard and chrome chair were new investments. The marble fireplace, held in place by two screws, was bought years ago in a junk shop. The old pine mirror frame was also cheap, painted matt black and marbled in silver and dark blue.

2

2 The south-facing
conservatory makes a sunny dining room, with the windows screened by fine blinds to let in maximum light. The chrome and glass dining table came from a shop selling seconds. In an alcove is a bust of Shakespeare set on a column – the bust actually comes from a garden centre and is cast concrete painted white and marbled. The column itself is painted cardboard, sponged in grey.

23

3

3 An aluminium loft ladder, on the other side of the living room, gives access to the gallery bedroom. The plain balustrade was handmade by a carpenter friend, who also built the bed and kitchen units. The trolley is a junk shop bargain. Plate glass shelves were added and the original bright yellow finish was covered with black Hammerite, a textured paint.

4 In the gallery bedroom a low bed is covered with a heavy cotton bedspread patterned with an ikat design, brought back from India by a friend. The television set is mounted on a swivel bracket designed for monitors.

A gallery – which remains in view of the main living area – needs to be kept free from clutter. In this apartment, where space is at a premium, a whole room has been devoted to storage.

5 The new kitchen layout was planned by a graphic designer friend. The floor is hardboard, painted black and then spattered white with a toothbrush. A marble slab from an undertakers' makes an unusual chopping board.

Before any building work begins, ask the contractor to provide a detailed specification – otherwise you may be charged extra for items such as fittings. If you are going to supervise the work yourself, plan to spend a considerable amount of time on site.

BACK TO SCHOOL

Pattern contributes a great deal to an interior – colour, of course, but also texture, depth and rhythm. Although many people are wary of putting a number of different patterns together, this converted Victorian schoolhouse shows how successful such an approach can be. Densely layered, but full of vitality, it draws inspiration from the designs of the past.

The owner, Graham Carr, a specialist in interior decoration and paint techniques, was looking for a disused chapel when he came across this village schoolhouse. As well as providing the large open space he wanted, the building featured Gothic detailing and a beautiful wooden floor, stained and restained over so many years that the surface had come to resemble tortoiseshell. Conversion was quickly and efficiently carried out by a local builder. Over a period of six weeks, the kitchen was refitted, the cloakroom turned into a bathroom, a false ceiling in the main room removed to reveal the supporting beams and a gallery built at one end to provide space for a bedroom.

After the building work was finished, the first decision was how the floor should be treated. The main grid of the design was drawn on the diagonal to add to the scale of the room; the colour and even the patches of wear of the original floor were incorporated into the pattern. White squares, painted in undercoat and then marbled, are thrown into relief by light and dark brown borders. Three coats of varnish and waxing make a lustrous surface.

The walls in the main room provided Graham with the opportunity to execute a large-scale stencil, with a motif derived from a seventeenth-century fabric design. In all his work Graham uses oil-based paints because of the richness and depth you can achieve with successive glazes. Here a thin undercoat provided the foundation for a glaze of stone colour. The stencilled design in grey-blue was covered with yellow varnish to give it an aged look.

Elsewhere in the house Graham's enviable ability to paint designs freehand is displayed in *trompe l'oeil, faux* panelling, marbling and fake tiling, making a rich setting for a collection of furniture, pictures and objects from different periods and parts of the world. Everything has been carefully assembled so patterns interact and complement one another.

1 The double-height living
room has a gallery, reached via
a nineteenth-century French
oak spiral staircase, bought
because it would take up little
room. The metalwork on the
stairs was decorated by
stippling bright peppermint
green over black with a dry
brush, to simulate weathered
bronze. The platform facing
was originally painted in a dark
rope pattern then toned down.

2

2 An antique Spanish pot,
at the far end of the living
room, is flanked by an English
chair and a *trompe l'oeil*
firescreen depicting striped
tulips, painted by Graham in a
morning. *Trompe l'oeil* should
always be executed quickly
and freely for a fresh,
decorative look; anything
excessively worked over
becomes flat and obvious. The
chair rail was moved down the
wall to suit the new
proportions of the room.

3

4

3 A quiet corner displays more decorative skills. The desk, a stripped pine kitchen table, is given a Gothic look by painting a quatrefoil design around the edge. Both the tin lamp base and tea caddy beside it were painted and gilded. On the walls, framed Chinoiserie panels serve as source material.

4 The fireplace makes a glowing focal point in the main room. Although the original building included a chimney, the fireplace itself and the surround had to be installed. Local flagstones extend out into the room to make the hearth; a profiled and gilded wooden mantelpiece supplied by the builder rests on two carved consoles from Portugal, secured by screws. Under the mantelpiece Graham has painted a design copied from Delft tiles.

Picking up the warm colour of the walls, a late eighteenth-century Portugese church hanging covers the chimney breast, sewn all over with metal sequins that catch the light. The circular hanging suspended with a vivid red ribbon is a Chinese embroidery; the oval panel suspended over the mirror to the left is a painted Dutch table top. Religious figures and a large Japanese plate decorate the mantelpiece; the chair is mid-eighteenth-century Portugese.

A tremendous sense of depth had been achieved by the layering of different patterns. It took time and experiment to achieve the right interplay of design. Graham, an avid collector of furniture and objects, tried out different pieces and arrangements, living with them for a while to assess how they contributed to the room.

5

Before painting a pattern on a floor, take detailed measurements of the room and work out the design to scale on graph paper. Each room has its own irregularities; don't rely on rough estimates. This floor was actually painted in two halves, moving furniture out of the way. For the amateur, it is best to clear the room completely and construct guidelines for the pattern before beginning to paint.

5 Another corner rich in details, to the left of the fireplace. A sheet of mirror glass is set in a Persian rope frame, which once surrounded a Quajar painting, and is itself decorated with tiny rectangular mirrors. Below, a semi-circular Portugese table made of carved and gilded wood provides room for display. On its top are arranged a Chinese lacquer box, silver-plated brass Tibetan beer cups and an eccentric candlestick, composed of an ivory column, oversized dish and unusual twisted candle.

An intriguing fragment from an Italian painting hangs to the left of the mirror; to the right is a French terracotta medallion. Reflected in the mirror is a painting by a Czech primitive painter. An ecclesiastical note is struck by the carved religious figure.

Before painting furniture or objects it is necessary to prepare the surface properly. Wooden furniture in good condition should be thoroughly cleaned and dried, and then undercoated. Metalwork must also be thoroughly cleaned and then primed with a proprietary metal primer to provide a good foundation for subsequent decoration.

6

Stencils are available ready- cut in a variety of different patterns but it is much more satisfying to make your own. Draw your design on graph paper and transfer to a sheet of acetate or to a piece of stencil board. Cut out the design with a sharp craft knife.

To apply a stencil, simply place the mask in position, taping it to the wall, and ponce through with a stiff square-ended brush. A special stencil brush is ideal for the purpose but even an old shaving brush will do. For a charming, uneven look, work quickly.

Plan the overall pattern carefully and stand back from the work from time to time to assess how it looks. Here the same motif was repeated along the chair rail but the rest of the wall was stencilled more irregularly. The design was taken from a damask pattern.

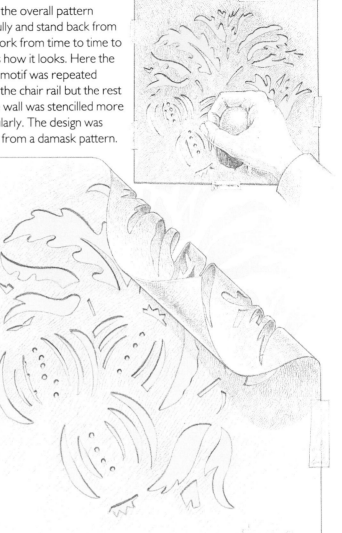

7

6 The gallery bedroom ceiling is decorated with a design copied from a ceiling in a twelfth-century Moorish palace in Majorca. The motif represents day and night and was handpainted for irregularity. To avoid a freshly painted look, a coat of varnish was applied and ragged off. The wooden screen behind the bed was painted brown, stencilled with a grey pattern, and then trimmed with gilded leather held in place with brass nails. Fixed to the screen are a pair of bracket lamps and two wooden statuary supports from a church, making ingenious bedside tables. A walk-in wardrobe reached via a door incorporated in the screen solves the problem of clothes' storage.

7 The walls of the hall were handpainted with a design taken from the Chinoiserie panel on the wall behind the desk in the living room (see 3). The background is a stone colour; a dirtied varnish was ragged off the top for an aged look. The Gothic cornice and dado panelling were both painted on using a simple illusory technique that involves opposing light and dark outlines to simulate the shadow cast by moulding. Deliberately crude terracotta and black marbling decorate the chair rail.

ART OF LIVING

The home of art dealer Hester van Royen and architect John Pawson is as rigorous an expression of minimalism as you could find anywhere outside Japan. A four-year stay in that country confirmed Pawson's taste for simplicity – even as a child he liked empty rooms. But while this immaculate apartment, the product of considerable structural and decorative work, is beyond most people's resources, it provides lessons particularly relevant for those on a lower budget.

At first sight, the absence of furniture, appliances and general paraphernalia might seem to indicate a drastic way of saving money. But the removal of these traditional reference points from view means that what is left – every surface from floor to ceiling – must be perfectly finished to stand the scrutiny. Apart from precision detailing in the plasterwork and flooring, this involved transforming the original rooms into a series of linked spaces.

Possessions are a fact of life, and however scrupulous you are about keeping them to a minimum you need to provide ample storage space to maintain your minimal interior. In this apartment whole walls have been fitted out with built-in cupboards. The cupboards are designed so that blank door fronts almost 'disappear' against the lines of the walls, making them indistinguishable from a plastered surface. Such accurate construction costs money.

Although in this case less is more expensive, economy and minimalism are not incompatible. In particular, it isn't necessary to embark on costly structural alterations to capture something of the same spirit. Making an anonymous space is a good way of accommodating eating, working and sleeping in the same area – essential if your home comprises just one room. In the same way, furniture can be vastly simplified to multi-purpose cushions and futons, easily moved from place to place or rolled up and stored out of sight. And the discipline of storing your belongings is a good exercise in rationalization. Paring down to the essential saves money, space and time on maintenance.

This is a family home, shared with Hester's daughter Phoebe and John and Hester's young baby. A constant need for tidying makes it a demanding environment in which to bring up children but one that provides a calm centre to life.

1 New openings link the living rooms. Walls were pulled around the bay windows to square off the alcoves; fine Venetian blinds screen the view. No more than a black hole in the plain white wall, the working fireplace is lined with Welsh slate. Together with more conventional chairs, zabuton, Japanese cushions, provide flexible seating.

2

2 The ebonized pitch-pine floorboards are carried through the whole apartment, polished to a soft shine that looks almost fluid. In the absence of cornices and skirting or baseboards, plastering is precision perfect. The walls appear to float above the floor – in a neat detail, the plaster is stopped short on a metal beading. These elements reduce decoration to the play of light and shade on plain surfaces.

33

3

3 A pillar in the entrance area forms the only curve in this rectilinear flat, making a pivotal point for the layout. To the right are the two main living rooms; to the left, down a corridor, the bedrooms, bathrooms and kitchen. Both sides of the wall dividing the corridor from the kitchen house floor-to-ceiling cupboards. On the corridor side these contain books and on the other side, in the kitchen, they contain cooking equipment and food.

The floor-level lights recessed into the corridor wall are actually fittings designed for outdoor use. At this low level they take full advantage of the reflective, fluid quality of the black floor.

Changing colours flash in sequence, provided by 'Sweet/ Suite/Substitute', a neon sculpture by Bruce Nauman, appropriately subtitled 'Art to replace your favorite piece of furniture'.

In this spare setting whatever is displayed on the wall must be of real quality since it immediately becomes the focus of attention. Paradoxically, more commonplace objects, such as household appliances, also acquire a new importance once they are taken out to be used, making art out of the everyday.

An unseen drawback of minimal living is noise. Ordinary furnishings, such as carpets, curtains, chairs and tables, do provide a surprising amount of sound insulation. Without them, sound spills from room to room, bouncing off walls, making private conversations impossible and dinner parties for four sound more like twenty. Pawson is considering applying insulating material to the walls, but this will be an expensive remedy.

4

4 Ultimate built-in kitchen:
a long blockwork construction covered with Resicrete, a textured non-slip surface designed for use on steel foundry floors, forms the central island for the kitchen. Inset in the top of the island are gas cooking rings or burners and a deep stainless sink with taps and spout dropped below the surface.

Industrial downlights, incorporating air-extractor fans to keep the air and surfaces dust and grease free, illuminate the work surface.

The wall of cupboards houses the oven, refrigerator, dishwasher, larder, cutlery and crockery. Like all the cupboards in the flat, these are made of MDF (medium density fibreboard), a modern material that needs no facing and is more stable than composite wood-chip board. All cupboard doors open flat on 180-degree hinges. These press open and shut –

eliminating the need for handles which would spoil the line of the wall-length doors. Inside the cupboards, the shelf depth is variable, so each shelf can be used to store objects one row deep only. This makes the daily task of tidying easier because one item does not obscure another or have to be removed when putting things away. The storage system is integral to the design of the whole apartment. If a shelf is narrower on one side

of the cupboard, in this case the kitchen side, it is wider on the other side, in this case the corridor where books are stacked.

The kitchen clock fronts the panel which conceals meters and fuses but keeps them easily accessible. Pawson would like to have hidden the neat row of light dimmers as well. In the centre of the panel is a recessed space for the telephone.

5

The discipline required for minimal living is nowhere more evident than in this stripped-down bathroom. All the cupboards are outside, so everything from towels to toothbrushes must be brought in when required.

5 Tiled from top to bottom in matt white ceramic squares, the main bathroom contains no cupboards, none of the usual paraphernalia and few standard fittings. In such spartan surroundings the grid of the tiles, whose width matches that of the floor-boards in other areas of the apartment, creates subtle pattern, and the pedestal basin and the pullout shaver mirror acquire a plain functional beauty.

Sculptural interest is provided by the chrome taps, towel rail and shower fixtures.

The window is covered by a narrow Venetian blind — carried from floor to ceiling to keep detail to a minimum.

Another integral feature is the built-in shower to the left of the window. Water from it is taken away via a discreet floor drain.

6 A hot tub is the focal point of the bathroom, a Japanese design made in cedar wood for aromatic soaking. In the Japanese way, the shower is used for washing and the tub for relaxing. The water is controlled by two chrome taps on the wall with plumbing concealed beneath the tiles. The wooden blocks on which the bath rests are exactly the width of the floor tiles and every tap, rail and accessory is in brightly polished chrome.

7 A cloakroom basin
specially designed for the
modern Barbican Centre in
the City of London is used in
the lavatory. It is recessed
fittings such as this which are
the key to minimizing impact
and maximizing available
space. The basin is set back
into the wall and has an
integral, concealed, toilet
roll holder.

6

7

*Almost as important as
flexible and spacious storage
in this minimal environment is
ensuring all utility pipes and
wires are unseen. This
requires careful planning since
any plumbing and electrical
work – which means not only
major work but such details as
the exact positions of lights,
sockets and taps – must be
carried out before any surface
work such as plastering or
laying floors is even
considered.*

37

WHITE LIGHT

White walls, white floors, white paintwork, white blinds. This brighter than bright Parisian apartment uses a simple stylistic device to achieve the purity of minimalism without spending a lot of money. As the previous apartment illustrated, the less you put in a room the better the quality of surfaces and decoration has to be. White, because it reflects light, tends to even out superficial flaws and provide a consistency of texture.

Marie Chaumette and Patrick Poirier, and their baby son Antoine, moved in to a filthy office and factory space two years ago, in what was once a tin and pewter factory. The two floors below were occupied by Marie's aunt and grandmother; her father had used the area where they now live as an office. It was a building Marie knew well since it had been owned by her family for years and it offered unusually spacious conditions for central Paris. But because of business commitments Marie and Patrick had to rely on their ingenuity rather than a healthy bank balance to carry out the conversion.

Structural alterations opened out the living area – the enlarged openings have not been fitted with doors so that light from the back of the building filters through to the north-facing front. One large room was partitioned to provide a kitchen and bathroom using an ingenious dividing wall designed to create a shower space on one side and kitchen storage on the other.

One of the problems of decorating a home entirely in white is, oddly enough, colour match. Whites come in a wide variety of 'shades', a function both of texture and the tints they contain. Popular white emulsion, for example, often includes a little blue to add 'brilliance'. Other whites may yellow with age. Here the purity of the wall finish has been carefully matched by the matt linoleum floor which extends right through the apartment.

Existing office cupboards have been incorporated with a finish of white paint and the few pieces of furniture were bought, found or inherited. The result is a beautiful and surprisingly comfortable apartment and, despite its austere appearance, a relaxed environment for their two-year-old child Antoine.

1 The living space is tranquil and restrained, yet comfortable. Fitted shelves in an alcove and tall wall cupboards – essential storage – were existing utility office fittings, painted white to blend into the background and style of the apartment.

2

2 Marie, Patrick and Antoine. They have invested in a few beautiful pieces such as this low table by Bernard Vuarnesson. Its ingenious design incorporates pull-out panels and display drawers. The blue cotton covers soften the lines of the sofas and add a subtle colour interest. They are also flexible; easy to change if a new colour is desired and easy to remove and wash.

3

4

5

3 Marie's collection of blue glass – old and new – adds a note of colour to the all-white living room. This collection includes many gifts from friends; the marble-topped table on which it is displayed was inherited. The blue glass light is by Italian designer Gae Aulenti.

4 This classic 'AA' chair was found abandoned in the street and fitted with a new pale blue cotton cover to match the

sofas. On the floor, silver bowls and lilies are variations on the theme of white.

5 An Art Nouveau fireplace, discovered in an antique shop, is a prized possession. Displayed in the almost empty area which acts as a transition between the living room and the rest of the apartment (see 10), it has been amusingly positioned against a blank wall to emphasize its original function.

Spare, rather than truly minimal, this apartment displays a few carefully chosen possessions, arranged so as not to interfere with the basic simplicity of the scheme. The clarity of style depends, first of all, on making do with the minimum of furniture. The owners, who run a business selling knitwear and other clothing made to their own designs, are trained to select and group objects effectively. Their philosophy is simple –

invest in a few well-designed and functional pieces.

Introducing vivid colour to an otherwise monochromatic space can be problematic. Here the pale blue of the loose covers provide a link between the white decor and the deep blue glass.

In simple surroundings, collections can also look out of place. The most effective solution is to group the pieces for impact. The collection will read as a single focal point.

41

6 The kitchen is linked to the living area by a large opening which allows natural light from the south-facing window and skylight to spread into the apartment. The unusual chair and stool – combining metal and wood and dating from the 1920s – were discovered in an antique shop in the Marais district of Paris – the same source as the Art Nouveau fireplace.

The floor, perhaps the most important element in any interior, is particularly crucial in a minimal environment. Its visual impact is enormous because of the amount of surface area it covers. Flooring affects many other aspects of an interior, too – sound, safety, texture, warmth and light. In this apartment the floor was a major investment and the first decision of any significance to be made by the owners. They chose the white sheet linoleum because it provided a strong, washable, stain- and scuff-resistant surface. Its reflective quality also adds to the sense of space. Warm and quiet underfoot, it makes a perfect surface for a young child. Apart from all these advantages, the aspect which finally decided them on their choice was the colour – a 'good' white without any undertones of yellow or blue. In an all-white environment any significant variation of texture or tone would destroy the unity. This white is a perfect match for the paint used for walls and ceilings.

6

7

8

7 A wall fitted with shelves
stores glassware and crockery
out of harm's way. When the
partition was planned to divide
one large room into a kitchen
and bathroom, rather than
build a flat wall, alcoves were
incorporated into the design
to accommodate different
functions (see plan on page
45). This made-to-measure
solution is more practical and
space-saving than bracketing
shelves on a flat surface.
Marie's preference for blue
comes out in her choice of
crockery.

8 The wooden work surface
in the kitchen – consisting of
wood sections like a butcher's
block and available by the
metre – rests on a basic
structure of breeze or cinder
blocks. This construction was
not only inexpensive but easily
carried out by the owners.
Sections hold the washing
machine and a freestanding set
of drawers. A loop of linen –
in traditional kitchen cloth
design – hangs on a wooden
roller to hide cleaning
products. The cupboards, like
the larger versions in the living
area and elsewhere in the
apartment, were part of the
original office fittings inherited
by the owners when they
moved in. Their simple,
utilitarian style works well in
this setting.

43

9

9 The bathroom was built from brick, faced with white ceramic tiles, to create this basic sculptural construction which houses the basin and bath. Setting standard bathroom fittings into a solid structure avoids awkward spaces which can trap dirt and give an uneven and cluttered effect.

Glass shelves fit neatly into a recess that was once a doorway and has now been blocked off. They provide unobtrusive storage for attractive bathroom accessories set off by a large mirror installed behind.

The curved perspex table, an Italian design, is one of a pair, the larger version of which stands in the living room.

One of the advantages of being able to plan the kitchen and bathroom from scratch was that the servicing for both could be incorporated, making a considerable saving in the cost of plumbing and the ease of its installation. Determining where to place the dividing wall that created the two new rooms meant taking a decision about how much space to allocate each. In the end, the simplest solution was adopted, positioning the wall to leave a window on either side so that both kitchen and bathroom could have the benefit of natural light.

10 A shower unit and lavatory closet were incorporated into the design of the partition wall which divides the kitchen and bathroom. Again, the basic construction is brick, faced with ceramic tiles. The uncurtained shower is raised on a platform to minimize overflow; the lavatory is suitably screened from the rest of the room. Unlike other openings in the apartment, the entrance to the bathroom is filled with a door for privacy.

The room adjoining the bathroom, viewed here

44

10

through the open doorway, is an almost empty space that makes a neutral transition between the different areas of the apartment. Although this room could have easily been incorporated into the living area by removing a wall, the effect would have been to run all the activities of the household together, increasing noise, losing privacy and sacrificing the atmosphere of calm that minimal living sets out to promote.

The plan shows the original layout of the factory and offices (grey) and the changes made by the present owners (red). These alterations consisted mainly of building partition walls and removing doors.

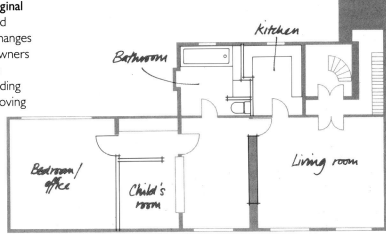

Kitchen

Bathroom

Bedroom/ office

Child's room

Living room

12

11 The workroom/office at the rear of the apartment takes up one wall of the bedroom. Absolute simplicity again provides the key to the design. A broad sweep of laminated wood fits neatly under the windows to benefit from natural light. Supplementary lighting is provided by the modern Italian desk lamp. The countertop is set at the correct height for working at a drawing board and is also well out of the reach of a child. Underneath, freestanding cabinets store drawing materials and office equipment.

Reached by a ladder, a narrow platform provides access to fitted storage, a leftover from the days when this area was originally a warehouse for the factory. The owners are now considering broadening this walkway to make a gallery bedroom.

12 A low-level bed occupies the opposite end of this room. Since clothes are stored in the platform section, the sleeping area can be kept free from clutter. It contains only the bed, with its bright cotton cover, a small, wooden chest, and a tiny curved, wooden stool.

The windows are screened with plain cotton roller blinds. Above, the sharp planes of a solid valance provide both a neat finishing detail and a counterbalance to the lines of the long, low radiator. Nothing has been allowed to intrude on the Japanese-style serenity.

A minimal approach suits dual-purpose rooms where the conflict between different activities can result in an unfortunate clash of styles. This room, with its simple functionalism, is designed to promote a good atmosphere for both of the uses it must accommodate.

47

SMALL IS BEAUTIFUL

The standard design approach when rooms are small is to employ a number of visual tricks to make the spaces seem larger than they really are. Using light colours, restrained patterns and a minimum of furnishing are all tried and tested ways of accomplishing this aim. But, as this scheme shows, there's more than one way to tackle the problem. Here the solution has been to acknowledge the scale and play up to it, making a warm and cosy interior that does not attempt to disguise the limitations of its size.

This tiny apartment comprises a bedroom, bathroom, hall, narrow galley kitchen and a living room no bigger than 3m × 3.5m (10ft × 12ft). A semi-basement with a small walled enclosure for a garden, it has no views to speak of. Before the present owner, Jenny Taylor, bought the flat, it had been completely decorated and fitted out in a muted colour scheme and quietly tasteful furnishings – the only trouble was that it was too formal for Jenny.

It takes a certain amount of courage to redo a recently decorated interior, particularly if the standard of finish is high, but this is what Jenny did. While she could only justify the expense on grounds of personal taste, there were certain practical advantages. Since previous work had been carried out well, she was able to take a purely cosmetic approach, saving time as well as money. Some of the existing colours could be incorporated into the new scheme; fitted cupboards were transformed with paint; the chintz living room curtains were sold.

Even though the temptation might have been to knock through a wall or two to open out the space, the arrangement of rooms leading off a hall has been kept to preserve the character of the apartment. Accepting that there wasn't much to look at outside, Jenny has made the living room inward-looking, with the detail of the window dressing standing in for a view. The rich red walls were designed to offset the tortoiseshelled woodwork, a treatment inspired by a pair of similarly painted lamp stands.

Redecoration only took three months. Jenny first moved in with just a bed, and much of her furniture remains in storage. Instead, priority has been given to display of favourite objects, emphasizing the 'jewel-box' atmosphere.

1 The vibrant living room is decorated almost entirely in red. Because the room is so small, much of Jenny's furniture could not be incorporated. An exception is the sofa, which has been reupholstered in red trimmed with green piping. The deep blue carpet, which runs throughout the apartment, was a compromise because the shade that Jenny wanted cost too much.

2

2 The marbled fireplace is an illusion in more ways than one. It consists of a wooden surround, marbled in grey-brown with white and black veining, applied to the chimney breast. There is no hearth – the suggestion of depth was created simply by painting the chimney breast black. The increased sense of space created by the large mirror and fireplace has been worth the sacrifice of seating room.

3

Austrian and festoon blinds are not the cheapest ways of draping a window. Their soft, full effect demands a considerable amount of material – ask an expert to help you measure so you don't underbuy. Unless you are very skilled, making the blinds yourself would be a false economy. A professional will ensure that the blinds pull up properly.

3 The window has been dressed with formal curtains and a festoon blind to compensate for the fact that the view of the back garden is nothing special. The curtains, which trail slightly on the floor, have been lined with the same glazed cotton used for the blind. The material for both curtains and blind is essentially plain to avoid an overly fussy look. The blind is drawn up to let in only a fraction of daylight – even in the summer the lamps are kept switched on.

The red display table in front of the window was originally a plain pine washstand Jenny had bought many years ago. She took off the back surround and then had the piece painted to match the walls. The finish was dragged softly to retain an impression of graininess.

The table lamp is one of a pair that provided inspiration for the entire scheme. Jenny bought the painted tortoise-shelled bases and liked them so much that she decided to incorporate other tortoiseshell details in the room – on the door and the interiors of the wooden display cabinets. Since tortoiseshelling is such a strong, striking finish, the rest of the colour scheme had to be equally vivid to set it off.

The lamps were trimmed to match the room, with cheap pleated paper shades and rich green and blue bows. Lighting is kept deliberately soft and intimate.

4

Dragging is a simple way of decorating wooden furniture or trim, giving a gently textured finish that hints at the graininess of the material. A thin glaze is applied to a suitable base coat and then, while the surface is still wet, a dry brush is dragged through the glaze, removing paint in fine parallel lines.

5

4 An ordinary circular table is transformed with a length of glazed cotton, printed in a paisley design that incorporates thirteen colours. It was an expensive purchase, but provides an essential contrast to the otherwise flat colour scheme.

The living room walls were colourwashed for a soft, slightly textured look reminiscent of silk. The foundation was a strong pink to give the top coat an added brilliance. An oil-based red glaze was then painted over the base, flipping the paintbrush from side to side to make the brushmarks obvious. The final coat was a transparent glaze which imparts a slight sheen to the surface. All the paint finishes in the apartment were carried out by professional decorators.

5 Wooden display cabinets, built into alcoves on either side of the chimney breast, were originally dragged in discreet shades of beige. The cupboard doors and facing trim were redecorated to match the walls, dragging the paint slightly to tone in with the texture of the colourwashing. Luckily, the material which covers the door panels was already the right shade of red.

By contrast, the shelves and interior of the cabinets have been picked out with tortoiseshelling. Since the patterning of this finish is so strong, it is best to limit its application to details such as doors and panels. Patches of warm brown and ambers with darked blurred diagonal strokes are the essential components of this finish.

6 The narrow galley kitchen, no more than a corridor between the entrance hall and back door, has been livened up with a strong colour scheme. The particular combination of bright yellow and inky blue was inspired by a photograph of Monet's kitchen at Giverny.

The open dresser provides useful storage for glassware and crockery. A favourite piece of Jenny's, it has been painted many times to co-ordinate with different schemes. Here it has been primed with several coats of eggshell and then dragged in dark blue. A plain Roman blind, trimmed with yellow, covers the glazed back door. The fabric, a remnant discovered in a sale, has also been used to make a small curtain to disguise the ventilator set into the top.

A selection of blue and white china plates and crockery makes a co-ordinated display.

7 In the entrance hall, from which all the rooms open off, a subdued striped wallpaper provides a neutral link. The dado panelling had already been dragged in cream and the paper was selected to match. Unusually, this has been extended over the ceiling – not an easy job for an amateur to carry out. A neat paper frieze above the chair rail and at ceiling height provides a finishing touch.

Black moiré satin ribbon, sewn into rosettes and pinned to the wall, introduces a Regency note. The pictures, like most of the ornaments and furniture in the apartment, were acquired secondhand.

Quality details make a real difference. Here brass light switches, matching the doorknobs elsewhere, cost considerably more than the ubiquitous white plastic variety but have the effect of making everything else look just as luxurious.

8

8 Unashamedly pretty, the bedroom is dominated by an old iron and brass bedstead. These beds are highly sought-after and can be extremely expensive, even in secondhand shops. Jenny found this one by placing an advertisement in a local paper. A little battered and rusty, it had been stored for some time in a garage with four others in worse repair. Although Jenny had to undertake to buy the whole lot this was still a cheaper option than buying a reproduction piece.

The pale yellow ceiling moulding and fitted cupboards have been left as they were when Jenny moved in. The walls, however, were repapered in a pink design.

Since the bay window overlooks the street, the view is completely screened with flat blinds covered with Austrian blinds. The two fabrics, both fairly expensive, are designed to go together – the motif on the roller blinds is taken from the pattern of the Austrian blind fabric. Over 20m (22yd) of material were needed for the Austrian blinds – having invested so much money, Jenny had them professionally made up.

The same material was used to make a cover for the pine chest set in the bay. A sheet of glass over the top makes a surface suitable for display. In a rather more ornate fashion, spotted cotton voile, looped and frilled almost like icing on a wedding cake, conceals a dressing table. It is attached around the edges with Velcro.

The candlestick lampstands were given new white paper pleated shades and trimmed with bows. Bows also trim an oval mirror, part of a collection of mirrors framed in barbola, a late 1940s' material that can be modelled like clay and painted once it has hardened.

DISAPPEARING TRICK

Tenants are often reluctant to decorate or make any substantial alterations to where they live. Even if the landlord gives you a free hand, the investment of time, if not money, may not seem worthwhile when your home does not belong to you. But in a city like New York, where the high pace of life means that some type of retreat is a necessity, it is important to spend the effort to make a place your own.

Alexander Vethers, an Austrian-born artist now living in New York, has been lucky on two counts. A chance conversation with builders working on his previous apartment led him to the discovery of this spacious 1817 federal house on the fringes of SoHo, a building whose age, architectural character and exposure to natural light make it a rare prize in Manhattan. He was also fortunate in that the landlady, who lives on the premises, had no objections to his plans for the interior.

Although the brownstone façade of the house was clad in red brick some years ago, the rooms are well proportioned and retain most of the original details, including shutters, floorboards, mouldings and a fireplace. Apart from extensive replastering to improve the surfaces, Alexander added nothing to the basic shell. The decoration was equally restrained. All the walls, ceilings and many of the floors were painted white, a strategy designed to make the space dissolve and 'disappear', throwing into relief the fine details and the few beautiful pieces with which the house is furnished. This treatment also reveals different textures, an aspect that has been exploited in the hallway and the distressed floor of one of the studio rooms.

The white, which has a translucent quality like porcelain, is not a standard finish but was specially created by a colourist who normally designs backgrounds for exhibitions. Since the colour constantly changes with the light, visitors are often surprised to learn that the same shade has been used throughout.

Overall, the atmosphere is one of Eastern calm. Sparsely furnished, with pieces chosen both for their practicality and purity of form, the space functions as a true retreat, free from visual distractions and discord.

1 The first-floor bedroom
overlooks the garden with its
Japanese magnolia and
flowering cherry. Curtains are
unlined Shantung silk,
suspended from thin wooden
rails. The floor was washed
several times with bleach to
lighten the tone. The bedcover
is a large piece of unlined gold
brocade; pillows are covered
in a Japanese fabric.

2

2 The staircase, with its
exposed brick wall, was dark
and gloomy. When the carpet
was taken up, a mosaic floor
was discovered on the landing.
Another happy accident
occurred when the walls were
painted. Although the stairs
were protected with sheets of
paper, paint still managed to
seep through. Alexander liked
the texture of the 'naturally
distressed' effect so much
that he decided to leave it as
it was.

3

If you rent your home, before embarking on major alterations check the terms of your lease or approach your landlord directly to establish what you are allowed to do. Few landlords object to basic redecoration but structural work will almost certainly require consultation. How much you do will depend in part on how long you anticipate staying, but some investment will make your time there more enjoyable.

3 The dining room on the first floor is linked to the kitchen by a double doorway. The floor was treated in the same way as in the bedroom, using bleach to tone down the warm colour of the pine.

Every other surface, as is the case in the rest of the house, was painted white, a shade specially devised by Don Kaufman, who designs colours for backgrounds of exhibitions. Many different oil-based pigments, including

purple and black, were added to pure white, and the finish is eggshell for a matt glow.

The centrepiece of the room is a Belle Epoque chandelier decorated with white glass lilies and bought from an antique dealer in New York. The dining table consists of two slabs of green Vermont marble on top of a refectory table bought at an auction. The little glasses are old German white wine glasses; the jugs are an American design.

4 The kitchen cabinets, with their cast-iron hinges and handles, were already in place when Alexander moved in. Instead of removing them, Alexander just painted the dark brown wood white to blend in with the walls.

Most of the kitchen equipment comes from nearby Chinatown, including a steamer and handwoven tray. The sleek modern kettle is a design by the American architect Michael Graves.

4

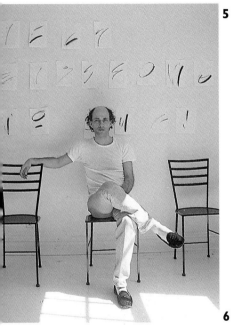

5

5

6

5 Alexander in his studio.
The ink sketches on the wall
are studies for big paintings
commissioned by Bergdorf
Goodman, a New York
department store, as
backdrops for window
displays. Their calligraphic
quality is in tune with the
Eastern simplicity of the
interiors – Alexander finds
that limiting his possessions
not only saves time on
maintenance but also inspires
the imagination.

6 The studio occupies two
rooms on the second floor.
This room, which faces west,
has wonderful light and is used
for preparatory work. The
floor was covered with several
layers of carpet in a fairly
derelict condition. When these
were taken up, the base was
found to be a mixture of new
wooden boards, lacking the
quality of the old pine
elsewhere in the house.
Alexander decided to paint
them white – not a solution

advisable for a more public
area, but since the studio is
only used by one person the
floor is easy to keep clean.
   Although the windows are
not curtained at the moment,
to gain the full benefit of the
natural light, the room
becomes very hot in the
summer.
   Even in the studio the
furniture has been selected
carefully to combine function
with beauty of form. Here the
two modern tables are by a

furniture designer friend,
Thomas Wendtland. In both
pieces, the legs are oxidized
copper, an aged green colour
reminiscent of Eastern
bronzes; the tops are polished
steel, so thin they appear to
float. A simple hand-thrown
pottery bowl is decorated
with a copper glaze.
   The metal chairs, like those in
the dining room (see 3), are
Italian, their design inspired by
the wrought-iron seats found
in European parks.

Although changes in the intensity and colour of light do not affect the execution of drawings, colour work is another matter. North light is favoured by painters because the strength of the light does not vary much throughout the day, making it possible to work over a longer period. The light is also cool in tone, enabling colour values to be judged accurately.

7 The second studio is an internal room on the same floor, an unusual five-sided space lit by a skylight. Since top lighting is the nearest alternative to north light, this is the room where Alexander works on his paintings.

The walls were sponged using a thin wash. Hardboard panels were discovered under the layers of carpet on the floor and these have been given a similar treatment. The uneven powdery texture is a function of the fact that the panels are stained with glue where the carpet was stuck.

The duck standing on the floor by the display of straw hats is a topiary frame for climbing plants.

Two walls of the studio are fitted with panelled closets with louvered doors. Linen and clothes are stored on one side; the other contains working materials. The house also has a separate laundry room with hanging space.

Textural variety is an important element in an interior. In this house, although the same shade of white has been used everywhere, the fact that it has been applied over different surfaces has provided a degree of interest. Although most of the walls were replastered, the brick of the hall was left exposed. On the floors different 'distressing' techniques have created subtle changes in rhythm.

ROOMS WITH A VIEW

Many city homes are understandably inward-looking, turning away from traffic and other distractions of the urban environment. Located in a quiet area off a main road, this small Victorian terraced house welcomes the outside world by setting up a series of external and internal vistas. Simple structural alterations, clever use of mirrors and quiet good taste have created a country atmosphere without sacrificing privacy or compromising the original character.

At the time of purchase several years ago the house was in fairly good order. With no major rebuilding required, priority could be given to structural changes that would open out the smallish rooms and create a sense of space. Because only limited funds were available, decisions had to be made about which alterations would be most effective.

On the first floor a partition wall was taken down to make a living room from the front of the house to the back. The sill of the sash window on the back wall was lowered to accommodate French windows, which open inwards, providing a view of the garden below.

Downstairs, the kitchen was originally housed in an extension, which was no more than a lean-to. This was demolished, making room for a patio sheltered by a retaining wall; a doorway was created from sash windows. The kitchen was relocated in one of the two basement rooms and, in a recent alteration, a partition wall alongside the stairs was knocked down to increase the floor area. Above the sink a mirror reflects the patio and back garden.

Equal care has been devoted to the outside spaces. The owner, Maureen Walker, planted a tree in the front garden which has grown up to soften the outlook from the living room windows. At the back, an old-fashioned climbing rose frames the view from the bathroom, and the patio functions as a true outdoor room, extending the kitchen out into the garden.

As a writer on design, Maureen comes into contact with a wide variety of styles and approaches but she has tackled the design of her own home without preconceptions. Colours are warm and light, and the rooms are furnished with a collection of favourite objects and pieces acquired over the years. The result is appealing and comfortable.

1, 2 The basement kitchen is a cheerful, sunny room lit by French windows that open onto a small patio. The units are composed of a cheap carcase fitted with MDF (medium density fibreboard) doors and painted with only one coat of eggshell to prevent them from looking new.

The cast-iron fireplace was stripped, sandblasted and bootblacked.

2

The most expensive, but effective, components are the synthetic marble floor tiles. Maureen went against manufacturer's recommendations by installing them in the kitchen but they have worn well.

Under a deeply set-back window, the cupboard houses the washing machine. The door panel is papered with a design that resembles Dutch tiles (see 2).

3 A spacious living room was created by taking down a dividing wall. The new room, with seating to the front of the house and a dining area to the rear, has been designed to read as one. A new oak strip floor, laid diagonally and extending into the hall, increases the sense of unity. Parchment walls and ceilings make a warm, light background; blue-grey co-ordinating the woodwork effectively pulls the room together.

The room is furnished with a collection of pieces from different periods and sources which nevertheless look as if they belong together. To promote this harmony, Maureen recovered the sofa and painted the chair.

4 The dining area occupies half of the new first-floor room. Because the garden couldn't be seen from a sitting position, the sash window on the back wall and the area beneath it were removed and replaced with French windows. These, like the pair in the kitchen, were bought from a salvage company.

Floor-length curtains made from cheap unlined Indian cotton were hung from an oversized wooden rail discovered in a junk shop. Another junk shop find was the narrow glass-fronted cupboard which serves as a cocktail cabinet.

Although there wasn't enough money left over to extend the living room cornice round the dining area, the grey picture rail serves as a link.

5

If you remove a dividing wall completely, rather than just creating an archway, the two chimney breasts lined up along one wall will act as reminders that the room was once partitioned. Although there was not enough in the budget to take out the second chimney breast, Maureen has disguised it by placing a cabinet in front (see 4).

5 Although the bathroom, like the kitchen, was totally refitted, it has a comfortably old-fashioned look. Tongue-and-groove panels were applied to make the dado and painted parchment colour to co-ordinate with the rest of the house.

The sink was salvaged from the Savoy Hotel in London and all the chrome bathroom fixtures are in a similar 1930s' style, part of a classic range available in department stores.

Because Maureen couldn't afford to have the walls replastered, they were covered with a pretty marbled paper to disguise the uneven surfaces.

Always consult an expert before carrying out any structural work on your home. Knocking down walls and enlarging openings can weaken the fabric of the building if proper reinforcement is not provided. It is also a good idea to have such work checked and supervised by an architect or surveyor.

SELF-ASSEMBLY

There is a particular satisfaction in finding a new use for what others have discarded. Skips or dumpsters, building sites and scrapyards provide good hunting ground for the urban scavenger, yielding a plentiful supply of sound materials, period details and the odd intact piece of furniture. Fitted out almost entirely from such sources, this ingenious kitchen, designed by an architect as a type of collage of architectural history, cost almost nothing to produce — except time.

Five years after Pedro Guedes bought his large Victorian terraced house, the kitchen is still the only room that has been completed. The house was a 'wreck' when he bought it, converted into bedsits and long-neglected. After putting right the effects of rot and damp, repairing floors, walls and roof, there was little money left for redecoration. But the design of the kitchen is not simply a case of making a virtue out of necessity. Constructing it in this way offered Pedro the opportunity to work with good-quality materials, explore craft techniques and express his ideas to the full.

The first step was to work out a fundamental approach on paper. Basing the design on some components that he already had, including three Victorian sideboards, Pedro developed the idea of creating an 'elevation', with the kitchen 'units' taking the form of different building types.

Although assembly was relatively quick, a lot of time was spent waiting for the right materials to turn up. Local building sites provided architectural details sympathetic in period and style; a scrap piece of marble came from a monumental mason's. Junk shops were scoured for likely pieces of furniture, none of which were used in their original states. Dressing tables, chairs, bedsteads and a hallstand were taken apart, turned upside down and reassembled as spice and plate racks, cupboards and shelves — even an Art Nouveau lift or elevator shaft grille was reworked as a *batterie de cuisine*.

Keen-eyed architectural students might be able to spot the various symbols and visual puns that were worked into the design as it progressed. An exercise in iconography that is both functional and richly decorative, this engagingly offbeat room gives new meaning to 'do-it-yourself'.

I The foundation of this unique 'built-in' kitchen is three Victorian oak sideboards, stripped, sanded and cut down to the same height to form a bank of 'units' running along one wall. A scrap piece of marble from a monumental mason's, cut and polished by Pedro, makes a luxurious work surface, above which pieces of junk shop furniture have been reworked.

2

2 An Art Nouveau wrought-iron grille from an underground or subway lift shaft has been suspended over the gas hob or stove top to act as a rack for hanging saucepans. The grille was stripped, polished with a wire brush and lacquered. Behind, strips of copper and brass were woven together in a design that represents flames. A sheet of black marble screwed to the wall makes a rich but washable surface.

65

3

4

Stripping paint or varnish from old furniture is normally achieved by immersing the piece in a caustic dip – a service now widely available commercially. However, for items with delicate carving or mouldings this may be a risky procedure since the solvent can bite deep. In such cases a gentler, if laborious, alternative is to use methylated spirit to dissolve the varnish and then sand with fine glasspaper and wire wool.

3 Above the gas hob, an extraction hood in the shape of a pitched roof is made of wood trimmed with a brass fender that was mitred, cut and soldered. The underneath was covered with many coats of gloss varnish to make it easy to clean. Pursuing the 'house of fire' theme, a torch-like candle holder has been fashioned from a dressing table leg surmounted by a brass reflector, cut from a sheet and riveted in place. The whole

construction projects from the wall on a piece of metal bedstead, whose end was cut with a grinder and forged with a blowtorch. Strings of candles and garlic hang from holes in the side.

4 To the left, a spice rack is actually part of a bedstead. Beside it, over the sink, a plate rack has been made from the back of a hallstand with the legs removed; the sides come from the back of one of the

sideboards. The dowelling and reed-shaped decoration are designed to represent water. Marble tiles inset in the top diffuse fluorescent lighting and, fixed to either side above the work surface, are brass Admiralty map-room lights that pull out on concertina brackets – two of the few items in the room that cost a fair amount of money. A porthole fitted with a glass brick provides a view of the staircase.

5

5 Storage for dried food is provided by a complex, temple like construction surrounded by various symbols designed to represent day and night. The shelving itself is part of a sideboard; supporting the pediment at the top are table legs cut in half to look like columns. The panel to the left behind the 'temple' has been painted black and covered with paste 'stars', while on the end wall a sun has been fashioned from a cut-out brass circle fitted with a reflector bulb, casting rays which are strips of stained wood. Above it, a shape cut out on a jigsaw casts cloud-like shadows on the ceiling. Every square inch has been similarly 'encrusted' with architectural symbols and meanings. Even the frieze running all the way around the kitchen shows characteristic deliberation. Since the room had been stripped of its original mouldings Pedro applied a plaster dental cornice. After this was in place, he decided that it looked too plain and uniform and devised the frieze to run beneath, composed of 15cm (6in) mirror tiles alternating with wooden 'triglyphs'. These were cut from pieces of floorboard and stained 'Greek' blue.

A gap between the two sideboards below the work surface has been filled with little sewing machine drawers for storing cutlery.

Fixing such a complex construction could have involved intricate detailing. Here the solution has been to line the walls with plywood so that everything could simply be screwed into place. Rather than conceal the method of fixing, expensive brass-capped screws are incorporated into the design.

RICH PICKINGS

When the present owner first saw this apartment it was run down and drab – carpeted in dingy grey, painted dull cream and filled with rubbish. But the proportions were generous and natural light flooded in from floor-to-ceiling windows. A young sculptor working from home, she almost made up her mind to buy the apartment on the strength of the light alone. The four spacious rooms and good location proved the deciding factor but also meant that the purchasing price left little in the budget for decoration.

Thankfully the apartment was structurally sound and required no major alteration or renovation. What it did need was a complete facelift. The result of the owner's efforts is a shimmering, eccentric interior with furniture and decoration functioning rather like props on a stage set, rather than fixed points of design. Although it is inspired in part by the faded grandeur of Venice and Versailles, the historical allusions are not heavy-handed, just deftly suggested in the details. Amusing and theatrical, the result has a lightness that can only be achieved when you know when to stop.

Three colours provide an important sense of unity throughout the apartment: soft, matt peach, aquamarine and old gold for accent. Everything from walls to vases conforms to this scheme – a rigorous co-ordination that looks expensive. The colours were carefully chosen to maximize the light, paint was specially mixed and every object was selected or decorated to conform; yet the colours are the last thing you actually notice.

Elyane de la Rochette works mainly with driftwood and offcuts from timber merchants, which she retrieves and coats in powdered pigments to create her sculptures. Her home reflects this delight in improvising and dressing up chance discoveries. She is also an original flower artist and designer of pottery and this is displayed in the unusual and exquisite arrangements – often just a simple vase containing one superb stem.

It has taken two years to 'finish the story'. Elyane describes her home as a 'dreamplace' full of surreal juxtapositions. Highly idiosyncratic but with a certain timeless quality, it is proof that a grand look doesn't have to be expensive.

1 In the spacious living room, windows are a dominant feature, elegantly draped with swathes of Indian handloom silk. This was bought in a whole roll from a dealer, costing a fraction of the normal price. The dining area has an unusual glass-topped 'Table with 13 legs', by furniture designer Mattia Bonetti, a friend of Elyane's. Its formal centrepiece reflects her interest in Japanese floral art. Simple folding garden chairs are dressed up with white cotton slip-covers.

2

2 The cornice moulding is detailed in real gold leaf. Running below it is a stencil, inspired by a detail from Versailles, which Elyane designed and applied herself using gouache — a type of artists' watercolour. This frieze was originally more extensive until Elyane decided that it looked overdone and painted part of it out. One example of 'knowing when to stop'.

3

Add artists' tint in small quantities to the base emulsion, stirring well. Apply a test patch and allow to dry before deciding on a shade – colours will be darker when dry. Make more than you need to complete the job so you can repair or add easily without the trouble of duplicating the shade.

3 The open-plan living area has pale, warm walls which make the most of natural light. Finding paint in the right colour proved impossible – the precise tone did not exist in the standard paint ranges available. Elyane chose the closest colour in a matt emulsion suitable for walls and ceilings. She then proceeded to correct the 'sweetness' of this pastel shade by adding colour tints in ochre, amber and black to create a 'chalky'

peach. Mixing your own colours demands practice and patience but, provided you have reference, whether it is a swatch of fabric or a photograph from a magazine, which shows the exact colour you want, you should be able to arrive at a match.

The sofa, bought at an auction and upholstered in velvet, makes a focal point – the only dark colour in the room. Its opulent curves are a favourite theme.

The sofa stands next to one of Elyane's sculptures – a piece of driftwood partly painted in a deep orange pigment and which houses a light fitting. The gold-painted Celtic cross installed in the hearth (see 1) echoes other 'gold' accents in the room, including the ornate, empty picture frames and the chandelier above the dining table, one of two bought during a visit to India.

4 **Classic, panelled kitchen** units were already installed in the apartment, raised on a platform at one end of the living room and on permanent view. All that had to be done was to paint them to match the walls. Since the kitchen is on display, functional objects are stowed away and open shelves are used for more decorative pieces. Appliances, refrigerator, washing machine and boiler are all hidden in a large cupboard to one end of the space. Utensils and crockery are stored in the cupboards, and shelves carry ornamental ceramics and glasses filled with bright powdered pigments.

Sanded and varnished, floorboards are often a harsh orangey-yellow – which could have ruined the subtle tones of this room. To achieve this pale honey colour the existing boards were whitewashed then covered in clear varnish. This is a cheaper solution than installing a new floor in a different coloured wood but it took a great deal of work. The floorboards were not perfect and required heavy sanding – a task which should always be done before any other decoration. Thoroughly sanded, the boards were given a light coat of whitewash which allowed the grain of the wood to show through. Four layers of clear varnish, applied over several days, finished the job.

5 The hall floor is in a muted pattern of Edwardian tiles, found in an excellent condition beneath an old carpet. The warm earth colours make a sympathetic entrance to the main living area. Two outsize stained-glass lanterns – left over from a set design – dapple the ceiling with soft patches of colour. Bare light bulbs over the kitchen counter are covered with gilt cherubs holding glass grapes – a Christmas decoration.

71

6

The kitchen nylon net measures 3.5m × 2m (4yd × 2yd). A standard sari is approximately 1.0m × 7.0m (1yd × 7½yd) but an alternative piece of decorative fabric could be used. In the bedroom, 25m (27½yd) of pleated cotton muslin was used – one full roll. Always buy more than you think you will need.

6 A simple idea transforms the view from the kitchen sink where a deep ochre and gold sari draped over a loop of cheap pink net adds a touch of glamour.

Cheap nylon net is sewn at both ends to form tight loops gathered on the curtain rod. The sari is pinned at one end and draped loosely over the curtain rod. The loose end is tucked up and pinned and the drapes are finely adjusted.

7 The main bedroom is dominated by a theatrical bed designed and made by Mattia Bonetti. A filmy wedding sari makes an unusual canopy draped over the green wrought-iron 'bed posts', the colour picked up in the chandelier. Light is diffused by pleated cotton muslin draped over the windows – again, bought in a huge roll for economy. One wall, not seen, is fitted with built-in clothes' storage.

Bedroom drapes are hung on a standard curtain rod with finials made from gilt tie-back bosses. First, straight blinds are made, seamed at one end to fit the rod. Adjusting draping as you go, use the finials to secure fabric and drape it as required. Elyane always improvises as she goes, pinning the fabric to the wall as necessary. The key is to have an excess of fabric so that it falls in generous drapes.

7

8 A collection of stoneware and vases designed by Elyane for her floral displays and made in collaboration with potter George Wilson. She poses with her little dog in front of the display shelves in her studio.

8

9

10

9 The all-white studio provides a neutral working environment. The floor has proved something of a problem. Originally sanded and painted with white gloss, it yellowed within six months and was redone in yacht paint, a slow-drying matt finish which does not discolour but has the disadvantage of showing every footmark. Paper Venetian blinds cover a storage area for tools and materials while a cheap textured fabric cut in kite shapes is stretched over the window frame in another simple yet imaginative treatment.

The display shelves cover the length of one studio wall. Pots and vases seem to float on their shelves, a solution seen in a Paris shop window. The movable glass shelves are suspended on fine steel wires, the whole construction counterbalanced by three white steel poles.

10 The second bedroom
remains unfinished. White
cotton temporarily draped
over the bed and armchair
helps to minimize the impact
of the bulky furniture. Two
books on either armrest turn
an old chair into something
more monumental.

In a design inspired by
Roman theatre, African lace
curtains sewn with paste
diamonds hang from strips.

11

11 The moulded ceiling
cornice has been painstakingly
picked out in silver water-
based paint and emerald
enamel, which took long hours
of concentration on top of a
stepladder. The ceiling is pale
blue and the walls a faded pink
– both colours created by
Elyane using artists' tints

The grand bookcase,
crowned with driftwood, is a
modern horizontal unit turned
on one end and draped in gold
cloth.

75

SHIP-SHAPE

Rooms can be replanned and redecorated, exteriors transformed and new services installed, but the one unalterable aspect of a house is its location. Even when fairly major problems exist, if the setting is really spectacular the investment may still prove worthwhile.

When Bob and Joan Bayley first saw this Long Island property, they were already in the middle of a renovation – the last thing on their minds was buying another home in need of conversion. Overgrown with weeds and uninhabited for several years, the house had no insulation, the roof leaked, plumbing and wiring needed replacing and tar shingles gave the outside an ugly appearance. Despite these disadvantages, the Bayleys could not resist the location – the house is situated right on the water's edge with marvellous views over a bay.

Instead of tearing the house down and rebuilding on the plot, they chose the cheaper option of extending and replanning what there was. Originally a one-room playhouse built in 1901, the house had been extended in the 1930s to include a bedroom, bathroom and kitchen. The Bayleys doubled the size of the living room and kitchen, integrated the main bedroom with an outside porch and turned a closet into a big bathroom. Walls were removed on the first floor and around the staircase to make the most of the views, and new double-glazed windows installed to increase light and air and improve insulation. Through careful planning, Bob, who is an architect, was able to carry out these extensive alterations economically, and at the same time retain some of the house's original character. The 1930s' windows replaced in the main part of the house were reused in the new conservatory and boards from the living room were taken up to extend the kitchen floor. The chimney was entirely rebuilt with stones picked up from local beaches and the house furnished with items from yard sales and similar sources.

With a semi-circle of decking extending out from the living room to face the water, the plan of the house resembles a ship. Wooden panelling in rough-hewn cedar, fishing pictures and strip windows emphasize the nautical theme. For the first time, the house is in tune with its setting.

1, 2 A new extension houses
the conservatory, which opens
off the kitchen (see 2). The
walls are standard timber
framing supporting 1930s'
windows removed from the
main part of the house. The
glazed roof is covered with
striped canvas awnings.

Since the room was originally
intended to be a greenhouse,
the floor at first just consisted
of cement blocks set into the

2

earth, spaced to allow plants
to drain between the cracks.
When it was decided to
integrate the area with the
kitchen, these were covered
with a platform of wooden
pallets constructed of framing
timber, which can be taken up
for cleaning.

Now the room where the
family spends most of its time,
the conservatory is furnished
with a homey collection of
chairs from yard sales set
around an old oak table.

3

3 The living room, extended to double the size, incorporates the core of the house, the original playhouse built in 1901. The old high-pitched roof has been lined in rough-sawn Western cedar, which was also applied to the walls and ceilings in the dining room and kitchen. This beautiful wood is particularly durable and needs no finishing or maintenance.

The pine floor was taken up to extend the kitchen and carpeting installed instead. The pale colour, a sandy beige, was chosen because the intensity of the sun would fade a deeper colour.

The entire room has been designed to make the most of the view over the bay. The original 1930s' paned windows were taken out and reused in the conservatory; in their place large glazed sliding doors were installed, which open onto a semi-circular decking made of redwood.

4 The dining room, which faces east, used to be entirely enclosed, but walls were removed and the staircase opened up (see 2) to integrate it with the kitchen.

This room is used principally from the autumn onwards when it becomes too cool to eat outdoors. It is decorated in the same unpretentious style as the rest of the house. The walls and ceiling are covered in cedar painted white on the ceiling to maximize light. The floor is original Southern yellow pine boards, a very hard softwood that is denser than oak.

The dining table is an old library table used for storing maps, with the drawers modified to increase leg room underneath. Framed fishing pictures hang on the wall, part of a collection found by Bob in an abandoned house. At the windows are Roman blinds trimmed with a contrasting border, made by Joan.

4

5

5 The kitchen resembles an oversized ship's galley. An island unit, built by local carpenters, is designed to accommodate all the main appliances and provide storage for glassware and cookbooks. The top is covered in bright Mexican tiles. On one wall is the sink; the other is fitted with a walk-in pantry. Beneath an internal window which connects with the living room is a marble countertop used for rolling out dough.

The cedar ceiling, like that in the dining room, was painted white after several years because the room looked too dark. Downlighters are recessed over the tiled work surface.

This floor also consists of original Southern yellow pine. Boards from the living room were used to extend the floor here; because of a flood they were saturated with salt which made the task of sanding very difficult. Polyurethane varnish has been applied to seal and protect the surface.

When you are planning an addition to your home, the siting of the extension is crucial. It should be positioned not only with regard to light, aspect and ventilation but also to work well with the existing internal arrangement. Here the living room was extended sideways, doubling the view, and the kitchen was lengthened. Both extensions were planned around the basic cross-shape of the house, minimizing changes to circulation.

79

6 The bedroom of eight-year-old Ryan is decorated with his choice of wallpaper. Roman blinds made by Joan, screening the light in summer and retaining the heat in winter, cover new double-glazed windows with hinged horizontal sections.

An Indian rug sets off the polished floorboards. Scatter rugs should be secured by underlay to prevent slipping.

6

7

8

7 Toys are easily tidied away in the wooden cubbyholes. Bought secondhand from a post office in Maine, these were originally used for sorting mail. More storage is provided underneath the cubbyholes by the two wooden chests fitted with rows of small drawers. Bob acquired these when he was an architectural student working on the renovation of a hospital. They were originally used for storing medical samples.

80

9

8 The master bedroom has sliding doors which open onto a deck over the roof of the living room extension, a vantage point with a sweeping view of the bay. The walls are painted turquoise, a shade used elsewhere in the house and Bob's favourite colour.

The pretty white wickerwork furniture gives a summery look. One of these pieces was found in the garage; the rest come from Bob's family.

9 The main bathroom combines old with new. The 1930s' pedestal basins came from a neighbour who was renovating his bathroom. The bottom of the old bathtub was rusted but, rather than replace it with a modern design, the sides were panelled in birch. The ledge around the tub lifts up to give access to a storage space. Wall-mounted opaque globes provide even lighting over the sinks.

The three stages of development from a one-room playhouse to a spacious beach retreat.

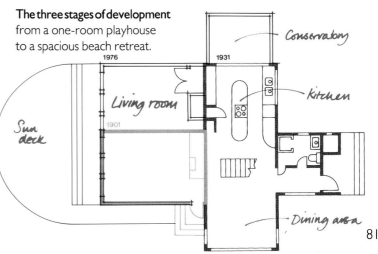

LATERAL THINKING

Calling in an expert can actually save you money, particularly when it comes to replanning your home. When architect Trevor Horne was consulted about correcting an extensive patch of damp and refitting a kitchen, he provided – for not much more than the original budget – the solution to both problems, together with the complete transformation of this small, ground-floor apartment.

Located in a large nineteenth-century building, the apartment had been poorly renovated in the 1970s, losing much of its character in the process. The living room looked out onto an untidy back service yard. At the opposite end of the apartment, the bedroom faced the street and was exposed to the sound of traffic. Connecting these two main areas was a disorganized jumble of hall, cupboards, separate toilet and bathroom, with only a small space left to accommodate a kitchen. With few windows and no through views, the whole apartment felt uncomfortably 'internal'.

What the architect saw was that simply by redesignating the main rooms and opening up a link between them the apartment could effectively be enlarged. And since repairing the damp meant removing much of the previous additions, this reorganization could be carried out very cheaply. In his scheme the apartment was turned around: the bedroom became the living room, the former living room became a study/bedroom; the hall was reduced to a vestibule; and a new kitchen/dining room created from the remainder of the space. Enlarging the opening between the living room and the hall made the most of the existing light and gave a vital sense of space. The new design was not only a logical use of the available area, it created a whole new room where the owner, Joyce Turner, could entertain her guests in more gracious surroundings.

This 'lateral' approach was also applied to the detailing. Radiators were plumbed in above the skirting or baseboards so that the new wooden floor is uninterrupted by pipework. Similarly, in the bathroom, skirting boards are recessed to align with the walls, maximizing the floor area.

The understated decor expresses the clarity of the design. A restrained use of luxury materials restores a sense of quality, fulfilling Joyce's original desire to 'live beyond her means'.

1 The kitchen is central to the new design. It is integrated with the dining area so that Joyce, who enjoys entertaining, can stay close to her guests. Neatly set into an alcove along one wall, the plywood units were built in three pieces in a workshop for a precision fit. The architect chose inexpensive materials for the basic structure. Then match boarding in machined pine was applied to the front of the cupboards to give the effect of solid wood but at only a fraction of the cost.

The oven is built-in with deep storage underneath for pans; on the opposite side the refrigerator is hidden behind a cupboard door. A pull-out chopping board gives extra counter space and a simple wooden rack drains wet crockery straight into the sink. The decor is restrained and formal, with quality materials providing a note of luxury. The countertop is a 40mm ($1\frac{1}{2}$in) black granite slab; the brass taps are from an architectural salvage company.

Simple uplighters, repeated on the opposite wall for symmetry, together with the grey walls, make the room read as an elegant dining area when the alcove downlights are switched off.

2

An important lesson of this scheme is to budget carefully so that details can be in a quality material. In this apartment, granite completes a cheap kitchen; the fine wood floor took up a large part of the budget and has more impact than any other element; the door hinges and handles are brass and the dining area was designed to accommodate a fine oak table which the owner already had.

2 Making this link between living room and hall took up a significant proportion of the budget. Since originally there was a standard door here the opening had to be considerably enlarged to take the attractive glazed doors.

Money and time were saved by first buying the Edwardian doors from an architectural salvage company and then making the opening to fit them. Decor is kept as simple as possible with plain white walls and a new oak strip floor, which serves to integrate the living areas. An entirely new sense of space is provided by the uninterrupted view through the flat.

Restoration need not involve a wholesale return to the past. Details such as doors, fittings and taps can suggest a period quality without the need for expensive alteration. Architectural salvage companies are excellent sources of period fittings and fixtures. Materials and workmanship are often high in quality, and prices are usually economical.

It is well worth the time to carry out a little research beforehand. An architectural library will have contemporary builders' catalogues, which provide good reference material. Studying a similar, but intact, interior may also help you identify the right details.

3 The bathroom is totally internal, but clever detailing and use of mirrors convey a sense of light and space often missing in a small room.

A mirror behind a downlit recess makes the most of glass display shelves. Flanked by tube lights, a mirror in a mahogany frame, together with old brass taps, give a period look to the room.

3

4

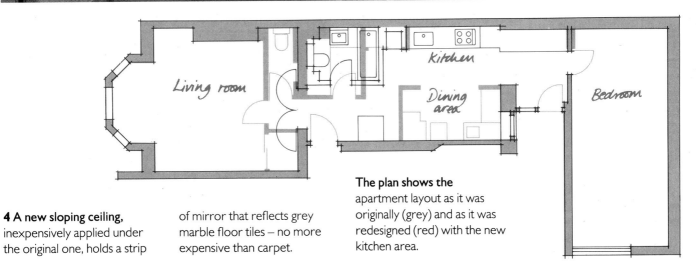

4 A new sloping ceiling, inexpensively applied under the original one, holds a strip of mirror that reflects grey marble floor tiles – no more expensive than carpet.

The plan shows the apartment layout as it was originally (grey) and as it was redesigned (red) with the new kitchen area.

Living room

Kitchen

Dining area

Bedroom

PAST REVISITED

There is often something self-conscious about period style. Re-creating the past can produce a museum, accurate in every detail but lacking vitality. Just as houses far outlast their original occupants, accumulating alterations and new functions throughout their lifetime, historical interiors are often the sum of various styles, woven into the composition at different times and by different hands. This Georgian farmhouse, restored and furnished with an eclectic collection from several centuries, has a special quality that usually only time can bestow.

When the present owners, Robert Kime and Helen Nicoll, bought the property, it was in a 'terrifying' condition. A low red brick building dating from about 1740, it had been empty since the war and needed extensive repair: at one point during the restoration work that followed, it was possible to stand in the cellar and see the sky. When tackling the renovation, Robert was guided by the fact that in Edwardian times the house had been extended so carefully – with matching quoins, bricks and mortar – that it is impossible to see the join. With the help of a carpenter-architect friend, Mary Lou Arscott, significant changes were made without compromising the strong character of the house or its charming irregularity.

This structural work was completed in three months; the problem of furnishing and decorating remained. With Helen, who writes children's books, working from home, and two children, Hannah and Tom, the demands of a busy household had to be taken into account. It was a welcome opportunity for Robert, an interior designer and antique dealer, to put his ideas into practice. Accordingly, the house contains a comfortable mixture of styles and periods. A strong interest in old textiles is apparent in the antique curtains and carpets, whose subtle patterning gives the rooms a great sense of depth. There is little that is in perfect condition; but the faded fabrics and signs of wear promote a relaxed, country atmosphere.

Overall, the approach strives for a harmony where no particular period is emphasized at the expense of another. This leaves open the possibility for the house to continue to change gracefully over the years.

1 In the garden room, 'Gothick' windows with stained-glass borders and copper glazing bars, which came from a country house sale, were rebuilt as sashes so they could be opened in fine weather. The walls were painted with a thin wash of grey and pink plaster over render; wires form a trellis for shade-loving climbers, planted in permanent beds. The floor

2

is a cheap variety of brick laid in a bed of sand and draining to a small earth bed. Since the roof is tiled, the room remains cool enough in summer for sitting in and dining.

2 A scullery, formerly the base of a back staircase, houses all the modern appliances to keep noise away from the kitchen. The sink is French, with an integral porcelain draining board.

87

3

Restoring a period home can involve extensive and costly repairs to the structural fabric; at the end of the day, modern materials and workmanship may clash badly with the original work. One strategy is to reuse old materials from demolition sites and municipal dumps, carefully matching colours and details. It is also worth enlisting the help of an expert with a knowledge of old craft techniques to plan and execute the alterations in a sympathetic manner. Here an eighteenth-century barn was rebuilt using the old bricks of the original walls to make a garden room (see 1), and the entire roof was replaced with Victorian handmade clay tiles. Elsewhere in the house, windows, fireplaces, bathroom fittings and cast-iron radiators came from similar sources – both cheaper and less intrusive than modern varieties.

3 The living room, formerly the dining room, is located in an extension built in 1904, designed and built to blend in carefully with the original house. All of the colours in the room relate to a worn eighteenth-century Indian carpet, now covered by another carpet in slightly better condition, and due to be renovated. Used mainly in the winter, the room has been assembled with layers of complementary patterns and tones, provided by details such as the Persian hanging, needlepoint cushions from a country house sale and silk velvet curtains. The walls are a neutral blue-grey, a shade that was specially mixed. The sofa cover, originally yellow, was dyed blue in the washing machine and then fitted damp the same day to prevent it from shrinking. Nineteenth-century brass picture rails, resting on brackets below the cornice, allow pictures to be

4

moved around without altering fixings.

In English homes, fireplaces are usually on exterior walls; in France the reverse is true. To add a fireplace to the interior wall in this room, Robert had to go to France to find one with enough depth to protect the wall from the heat of burning logs. The simple white marble surround, however, is not typically French in design and suits the plain style of the architectural details.

4 A comfortable living room, which forms the other half of the large kitchen (see 5), opens off the hall and main stairway. Wall-to-wall carpeting in cheap coir matting makes an economical and practical floor throughout the main living areas; its warm, textured appearance is also a subtle foil for antique carpets and rugs. The rather battered rug in front of the fireplace in this room was bought at an auction. Although its sunburst

pattern is rare, the rug was affordable because of its less-than-perfect condition.

The seventeenth-century stone fireplace was added and a worn leather-covered club fender installed as a hearth guard. On either side of the hearth are 1930s' Lloyd Loom basket chairs with unusual solid wood armrests and legs.

To the right of the door hangs a large portrait of Helen, painted by a friend, Mark Wickham. In the picture Helen

is sitting at the marble-topped kitchen table, with the sitting room in the background, a view within a view which enhances the intimacy of the room.

Robert admits to being dissatisfied with the wall colour, a brownish terracotta which is rather dull at night. Rather than choose the paint first, he waits until he has decided on the furnishings and then selects a plain, complementary background.

5 The kitchen/living room (see 4) is the hub of the household. Formerly the main drawing room, this generous space accommodates the needs of a busy family. On the wall to the left of the new back door is an Aga; in front of this is an Irish vegetable table whose top is a marble slab, 2.4m × 1.5m (8ft × 5ft).

The old dresser, which takes up the entire length of the back wall, was originally even longer but was cut down to fit into the space..Shelves hold crockery, jugs and glassware, while the drawers below provide storage for everything from bread to mending.

The windows have been left uncurtained. In the summer, a mass of climbing plants on the outside walls filters the light. The flagstones which make up the floor were originally part of a city pavement.

6 The bathroom, down a short flight of stairs from the master bedroom (see 8), combines utility with comfort. Pink and white patterned wallpaper makes a pretty background for a collection of 'sailors' valentines', shell pictures incorporating love mottoes made by sailors in the West Indies to give to their sweethearts. The curtain is eighteenth-century crewel work; the towel rail and basin are secondhand.

7 A modern porcelain bathtub has been panelled with Edwardian mahogany salvaged from a local bank. A satinwood wardrobe makes a handsome linen cupboard.

91

8

The conserving spirit of recent times has led to a renewed appreciation for all types of artefacts from the past. Today bargains are rare and the high demand for good-quality pieces has meant that furnishing your home with a collection of antiques is an expensive option. However, this can still be affordable if you are prepared to compromise on condition and accept fading, fraying, tears and other signs of wear.

8 The master bedroom is dominated by an nineteenth-century bed with an original chintz headboard. The cotton bedcover is 2.4m (8ft) square, hand-knitted by Robert's mother to an old pattern. The satinwood wardrobe, like the wardrobe in the bathroom, is by Holland and Sons, leading English cabinet-makers of the early nineteenth century.

The warm, natural colours again relate to the tones of the rug, a nineteenth-century

Ziegler design. The pale sand colour on the walls was achieved by adding tints of burnt umber to a neutral base.

9 The larger of the two spare bedrooms has been decorated and furnished in an Arts and Crafts theme. The walls are papered with Willowleaf, a William Morris design that incorporates six different colours; the Pre-Raphaelite watercolour panels depict the seasons.

10 In the second spare bedroom, a half-tester bed is hung with nineteenth-century chintz matching the curtain fabric. Framed needleworks are displayed on the wall.

Spare rooms often accumulate pieces that do not fit in elsewhere. Here as much care has been spent furnishing the guest rooms as the rest of the house – if you have room for overnight visitors it is worth providing a good welcome.

9

10

Most of the curtains are antique. Like the rugs, these were originally in fairly bad condition but have been restored, lined and remade by a talented needlewoman, Margaret Thompson. They have much more integrity than modern reproductions of period designs. Many of these fabrics incorporate as many as twenty different colours and fit easily into any scheme. In modern printing, each colour adds significantly to the cost per metre, so it is rare to find such subtlety. The vegetable dyes used to print these old designs also fade gradually, achieving a mellow quality with time; modern chemical dyes are apt to discolour quickly, fading out of synchronization with each other so the print loses its original tonal values.

EMPIRE LINE

With space at a premium, many Manhattan apartments consist of no more than a single room that typically has to accommodate living, eating, sleeping and even working. But as this converted loft shows, there is no need to sacrifice style or comfort when every square foot counts.

This fourteenth-floor apartment is part of a recent co-op development of a light industrial building dating from 1928. Located on the fringes of the garment district, with windows facing south and west, it has good views of the Hudson River and Empire State Building. The owner, Ed Carroll, felt that the sunny aspect could stand strong colours and an important part of the scheme is the dramatic use of mauve-grey and black.

Like many such conversions, the apartment retains hints of its utilitarian past, visible in the sprinkler system, concrete and steel beams and minimal detailing. To soften this rigidity somewhat, Ed, who is an architect, incorporated curves into the design in three places: in the kitchen, flanking the entrance hall, and to one side of the fireplace.

The curves also serve another function – to provide a more sympathetic setting for a collection of antiques, all of which are French Empire in style. This restrained style, which developed in France in the early decades of the nineteenth century, is characterized by classical simplicity, with plain shapes, gentle curves and sparse decoration.

But not everything in the apartment is an antique. There is a 1940s' sofa, a modern high-tech trolley, a Marcel Breuer chrome chair, and a round glass-topped table from the 1930s, coexisting happily with the earlier pieces. What they all have in common is a certain purity of line, which suits the character of the loft space.

Essentially one room, with a built-in kitchen and a separate bathroom and dressing room, the area must serve many different purposes. There is even a home office, equipped with drawing board and filing cabinets, set up in one corner. Eventually this will be moved upstairs when Ed completes the studio he is building on the roof. Even without this extension, however, the clarity of style, confident colour scheme and fine lines of the furniture give this apartment a gracious quality that belies the pressure on space.

1,2 The kitchen consists of a freestanding counter screening appliances built in under an enamelled steel top. The counter is a wood construction faced in black formica; its curved shape is repeated in the design of the canopy, made of plasterboard or sheetrock.

Strips of mirror on the cabinet doors over the worktop reflect the recessed downlights and the river view

2

from the living room windows, creating an illusion of depth. Behind the counter, drawers with chrome handles give ample storage space for cutlery and kitchen equipment. A decorative flourish is provided by the pair of ornate lamps, discovered in a Salvation Army sale. Their gilded plaster bases were painted to match the walls. The area behind the kitchen houses clothes closets, a bathroom and dressing room.

95

3

When the floor area is small, the walls assume much more importance as display spaces, since collections of objects on tabletops or similar surfaces would introduce a distracting degree of clutter. In this apartment carefully selected and arranged pictures have fulfilled the need for decoration without taking up usable room. These have been grouped with an eye for form and colour as well as for their content.

3 An antique French settee is positioned against the wall to the left of the kitchen counter. It is upholstered in Kelly green moiré silk, a vibrant colour echoed in the painting of rowers by Edward Melcarth, a popular American painter of the twentieth century. The framed drawing directly above the settee is a Melcarth cartoon for a painting and shows workmen at a lunch counter in the manner of da Vinci's *Last Supper*.

The success of this scheme owes much to the use of strong colours. Ed's previous apartment was decorated all in white to brighten it up; here, because the sun beats in constantly through the south- and west-facing windows, he felt that bolder colours would be more appropriate. Although the original concrete ceiling is painted white, an unusual shade of mauve-grey was chosen for the walls and structural beams. Ed came

across the colour when he was looking through manufacturers' sample cards and the paint was mixed up to a formula by the supplier. The paint is oil-based eggshell, with a slight sheen. Its reflectivity increases the tendency of the colour to change with the light.

Equally dramatic is the choice of flooring. Heavy-duty 'battleship' linoleum in black runs right through the apartment.

4

4 The main living area measures only 7.6m × 7.6m (25ft × 25ft) yet must also accommodate office and sleeping areas. A collection of French Empire-style furniture, together with sympathetic modern pieces, provides a consistency that prevents the room from disintegrating into conflicting spaces.

The industrial windows were originally barred with heavy steel grilles which were removed during the conversion of the loft. The floor-length white curtains are made of heavy artists' canvas bought at an art supply shop. The plain headings and stiff folds give a classical, sculpted look almost like a series of columns. Other touches of white come from the Italian bedspread covering the Empire sofa and the hide rug, alleviating the dark decor.

Since this apartment is on the top floor of the building it was a simple matter to install a fireplace. A steel flue was placed on the end wall, the whole construction encased in plasterboard. One corner of the chimney breast was rounded off to soften the angularity of the room. Above, a marbled clock rests on a painted plywood plinth. Two other plinths above the white sofa support gilded bronze Empire lights. The 1930s' table in the foreground comes from Ed's family.

When different activities have to be catered for in the same small area, certain approaches can ensure that the space still reads as one. Strict colour co-ordination is important; a degree of disguise can also help. Here the kitchen has been decorated to blend in with the living area, with the more functional side screened by a counter. Similarly, the sleeping area contains a French sleigh bed, in keeping with the rest of the room.

7 On the roof, Ed leans against a wall where a spiral staircase will eventually link the living room with the new studio. The bottom of the stair will emerge where the plan file is now.

5 An office occupies one corner of the main room, a compact but well-equipped area from which Ed runs his architectural practice. Desk space is provided by a 3m-(10ft-) long table against the partition wall, with a counterweighted drawing board at right angles to it. Behind, a metal plan chest or file stores architectural drawings flat. The antique French mirror on the wall is positioned exactly opposite the mirror over the fireplace (see 4). The large etching of Roman aqueducts is by Piranesi, an eighteenth-century Italian architect and archaeologist, while the model above is of the studio.

6 The 'bedroom' consists of a French sleigh bed from the 1830s, set under the windows. A bedside table is another antique – an antique French drumtable – while the mirror at the end of the bed dates from the same period but is American. The chrome chair upholstered in pony hide was designed by Marcel Breuer, a prolific Hungarian-born American architect and furniture designer. Although this design dates from the 1920s its simple lines work well with the older pieces.

The wall behind was designed to provide integral shelving for books and ends with a curve, repeated on the adjacent wall (see 2).

In a multi-purpose area, a degree of flexibility is important. A simple modern trolley and filing cabinets on castors can be moved from place to place as the need arises. These functional objects nevertheless fit in with the colour scheme – either black or, in the case of the wooden filing cabinet in the kitchen used for storing tools, painted to match the walls (see 1).

HOME
FROM HOME

A place in the country is everyone's idea of the perfect weekend retreat, offering respite from the bustle of city life and the insistent ring of the telephone. Second homes, once only for the rich, are commonplace today, and demand is high for small cottages and farmhouses within easy reach of major centres. But although estate agents and realtors like to paint a rosy picture of idyllic hideways, unless you approach the purchase with as much care as if it were your only home, the result could be both an organizational nightmare and a constant drain on your finances.

This small, two-storey Regency villa, the second home of two busy professional people, highlights many of these practical considerations. The first, and perhaps most important, factor is location. Although Alison Cathie and Paul Whitfield were not specifically in the market for a country home, they spotted this farmhouse while visiting friends nearby. In a small village set in rolling countryside, yet minutes from a main road and busy train station, it provided a perfect blend of rural charm and accessibility.

Like many such properties, however, it was in poor repair. Rather than approach the renovation piecemeal – turning what should be time off into a protracted exercise in DIY – local builders were hired to carry out all the structural and decorative work. A friend and talented decorator, Susanna Cornwallis, who lives nearby, took responsibility for the organization of the restoration – and three months later the house was ready.

As far as style and decoration were concerned, the owners were keen to avoid a self-consciously countrified look; neither did they want the house to end up as a repository for ill-matched left-overs. Opting instead for a cool simplicity, as refreshing as the view, they have created a light and spacious interior where favourite antiques and new acquisitions blend comfortably together. Domestic arrangements ensure that time spent at the house is enjoyed to the full, not taken up with household chores.

Second homes present many opportunities for making false economies. Through careful planning and strict budgeting, this house has been designed to provide its owners with a year-round welcome.

1, 2 The dining room is integrated with the kitchen to make a good area for entertaining. Plain white walls maximize the feeling of space (no room is bigger than 4m × 4m [12ft × 12ft]). A clear duck-egg blue, used on the woodwork, and curtains patterned with a design of leaves and cherries, suggest a fresh country atmosphere. Pictures are restricted to prints and watercolours, the

2

right tone and scale to be effective on plain walls.

The dining table, a simple pine affair, is covered with a tablecloth in a paisley pattern.

The new strip floor in Douglas fir was the result of much research. Looking for a practical but warm surface, the owners decided on wood after seeing a similar floor at a friend's house. It cost little more than tiles, but will last a lifetime and improve with age.

101

3 The kitchen, viewed from the dining room. To enable more money to be spent elsewhere, the old kitchen units were retained. These were cut down to size, cabinet doors gessoed and simple frames applied which were dragged in duck-egg blue. A new hardwood draining board was supplied by the builders and a deep but compact Belfast sink added.

4 The oil-burning stove which heats the house was already installed but its location was changed to improve the arrangement of the rooms. Above, saucepans hang from a curved rail forged by the local blacksmith, saving storage space and time spent doing the drying.

The hallway is viewed through a new archway which repeats the curve of the fanlight over the main door. The quarry-tiled floor was restored by scrubbing it with wire wool. To protect the surface, the tiles were waxed – polyurethane varnish would discolour and chip.

Equipping a second kitchen can be expensive but is essential if entertaining is a priority and time is not to be wasted carting boxes of utensils back and forth. Here money was saved because much of the equipment was actually surplus, left over when Alison and Paul married and amalgamated their possessions. The saucepans come from the galley of a boat they once owned.

3

4

5

6

5 Upstairs, in the main bedroom, grey and white decor creates a peaceful atmosphere. The floorboards are coated with many layers of white paint and covered with a cotton dhurry. Alison visited a factory to choose the bed, a cheaper option than buying one from a department store. An embroidered Victorian table cover, a present from Paul's mother, dresses up a plain cotton bedspread. Instead of a bedhead, an antique carved panel is screwed to the wall. This was once the front piece of a walnut Florentine chest of around 1600.

6 In the living room, the curtain fabric with its pineapple design was the starting point for the colour scheme. The pineapple, a popular Regency motif, is also a sign of welcome. The wickerwork chairs were the most comfortable Alison and Paul could find; the Chinese blue of the cushion covers is echoed by the Delft pottery on the mantelpiece. Cleaning restored the original Bath stone fireplace; a new ceiling moulding was added for architectural detail.

Without careful planning a second home can mean double the housework. Before the final contract was signed, Alison secured the services of someone local, who takes complete care of the house during the week and is on hand if any problems arise.

103

LIVING MEMORY

Collecting furniture and objects from the recent past has become a popular and profitable pastime. You can still find pieces of real quality from the early decades of the twentieth century, mixed in with all kinds of junk in antique markets and secondhand shops. Much cheaper and more plentiful than genuine antiques, such items require little renovation and have years of life left in them.

This Paris apartment, the home of cartoonist Fernand Zacot and Murielle David, is furnished entirely with pieces from the 1930s. To anyone familiar with the classic era of Hollywood films, this period has a great nostalgic value. But Art Deco, displaying a fascination with the streamlined technology of the machine age, represents the beginning of modern design, and the bold, crisp geometry and use of materials such as polished chrome and glass mean that it still has vitality today. Although the period has become very popular, with good examples increasingly sought after, by avoiding established dealers Fernand was able to fit out the whole apartment for no more than the price of a new sofa. The starting point for Fernand's interest in the 1930s and in collecting was a polished brass standard lamp, which the previous tenants had left behind when they vacated the apartment. After taking on the lease, he discovered a matching chrome lamp in a market and simply carried on from there, visiting the stalls at Clignancourt and the sprawling open-air market at Montreuil to hunt down bargains. Since Paris still ranks as the world flea market capital, good pieces were not difficult to find and the collection built up quickly.

The apartment itself, typical of the neighbourhood, is on the top floor of a building dating from the turn of the century. Apart from painting the walls white, Fernand has not changed anything. With an original parquet floor and details such as the *meuble cheminée*, a built-in fireplace, it makes an appropriate setting for the collection.

Every item, from lamp shades to the hallstand, is rigorously in period – and there are no reproductions – a consistency that generates a unique atmosphere. But this is no museum: everything is intended to be used as well as appreciated and the odd sign of wear is not a cause for concern.

1, 2 In the living room,
French windows with stained-glass borders are flanked by corner cupboards, one of which is actually a *meuble cheminée*, a built-in fireplace. This original feature goes right through all the apartments in the building.

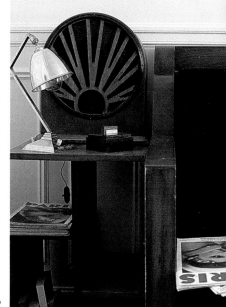

2

Against a plain white background – even the curtains are white – is set a collection of furniture and objects dating from the 1930s. The polished brass standard lamp, left behind by the previous tenants, was the inspiration for the scheme. The phonograph was a present from Murielle; the little cabinet beside the sofa, with an angled chrome reading light and radio on top, belonged to the former occupants.

3

4

3, 4 The dining room and living room are linked together by original double doors, making a through view to the small adjoining balcony. Since the total area of the apartment only comprises 70 square metres (754 sq ft), the large French windows and the double doors which connect the two main rooms provide an important sense of space.

All the architectural detail in the apartment was intact, making a traditional setting that, while not strictly in period (the building dates from 1900), is nevertheless sympathetic in character to the Art Deco furnishing. All the walls, together with plasterwork mouldings, woodwork and door and window frames, were painted white – an essential neutral background when the emphasis is on the design of the furniture.

By strictly limiting your choice to one period and style, co-ordination is easy to achieve, even when pieces come from different sources. The characteristic Art Deco materials, light veneered wood, polished chrome and glass, provide a ready-made harmony of tone and texture. The forms, too, complement one another. The rounded-off corners of the dining chairs and table echo the design of the marble-topped sideboard with its stepped edges.

Although there are now many shops specializing in 'retro' styles, it is cheaper to avoid established dealers and travel further afield to markets and auctions. Here the problem can be the sheer volume of material. The solution is to prepare for the search by spending some time in basic study of the period that interests you. There are many good reference books which make the task of sifting through that much easier.

5

5 Fernand in his study.
The Art Deco theme is carried right through the apartment. This small study, equipped with a period writing table and swivel desk chair, is where Fernand, who works at home, sketches his cartoons. The apartment also has an attic, which is used as a studio for colour work and airbrush rendering.

The portraits on the walls, which also come from flea markets and were picked out because they looked intriguing, emphasize the atmosphere of nostalgia. The clock in the chrome case on the mantelpiece is part of a collection – others are displayed on the mantelpiece of the *meuble cheminée* in the living room. Not all of them are in working order.

Because the furniture only dates from fifty years ago and the materials are good quality, most pieces have worn well and required little in the way of renovation. Although some of the armchairs are not quite stable, accuracy of period is more important to Fernand than perfect condition.

Most of the larger items were found quite quickly, but Fernand was also prepared to wait for the right details to turn up. A lamp base bought one year was finally completed the next when Fernand discovered the right shade to go with it.

6 In the entrance to the apartment, a chrome hallstand fitted with a mirror displays all the characteristic qualities of Art Deco. The chrome uplighter to the left, matching the living room lamp, was the first piece Fernand bought.

The original parquet floor runs throughout the apartment, its mellow surface complementing the warm tones of the furniture. No rugs have been added, preserving the sense of space.

6

ILLUSIONS OF GRANDEUR

If your home has problems that can't be solved merely by a change of style, it is often worth considering spending the money to alter the structure. This can open up more than just the possibility of extra space and suggest a whole new way of looking at your home.

When Paul and Cathy Hodgkinson moved into their top-floor apartment, it was dingy, dark and cramped. So much needed to be done in the way of decoration that it was difficult to see where to begin. As an architect, Paul's first response to these problems was to remove the ceiling in the main room and install skylights in the roof. This simple alteration not only transformed the small attic room by giving it height, light and space but also provided both the inspiration and the extra room they were looking for.

Removing the ceiling introduced daylight into the main room, improved its proportions, and allowed a high-level platform to be built under the eaves, making a much-needed work and storage area. It also revealed the classic shape of the end wall, rather similar to the façade of a Greek temple. To Paul, this suggested a unifying — and architectural — theme for the main area of the apartment.

Appropriately, with a limited budget and constraints on space, the design relies on flat, applied decoration. Specialist paint finishes and mock columns combine to tell the story wittily and economically. The walls were spattered, the 'rusticated' stonework effect and pediment simply achieved by masking out with tape. The columns, constructed entirely of MDF (medium density fibreboard), function either as bookcases or conceal side lighting; the same shapes are repeated on the opposite wall as decorative detail.

Colours were chosen to accentuate the tricks with scale. Extensive use of cream makes a warm, light background. By decorating the mirror, fireplace and columns to match the walls, sculptural interest is added without sacrificing any tonal harmony. As an important counterbalance to the new height, the solid furniture and column bases are black.

A few quirks liven up the formality. The spattered 'stonework' and 'pediment' slide around corners, poking fun at the symmetry. And peering down from a beam, gargoyles introduce a sense of medieval mischief.

1, 2 The living room was transformed from a cramped attic to this stylish and airy studio with its classical architecture theme reflected in shapes and textures. Removing the ceiling to reveal the slope of the roof and the structural beams defined the room and inspired the decorative treatment. The various paint finishes are described on the next page.

2

The massive furniture, set on a cream carpet, provides some visual weight to counteract the new height. The sofas and large tables were specially designed and made – an option which doesn't have to be expensive. They are constructed so that they can be taken apart – useful for negotiating the 87 stairs that lead up to this apartment. The blockboard coffee table rests on solid ash balls turned on a lathe.

3 Two plaster gargoyles – reproductions from carvings on Lincoln Cathedral in the east of England – are picked out by an uplighter. The gargoyles and light fitting were then spattered in mock stone shapes. This picks up the effect of rustication – an architectural term for designs which reflect classical stonework – elsewhere in the room.

3

4

4 A high-level study is reached via a 'Kee Klamp' ladder and has an iron balustrade. All the ironwork was painted with black oil-based paint for a high-gloss finish. The lines of the Italian chairs and 1930s' pedestal ashtray, painted black then spattered, provide more graphic interest. The mezzanine is large enough to contain a desk and filing cabinets or to provide a sleeping space for guests.

Spattering can be used to create an interesting textured effect like old stone. The shapes for the 'stonework' pediments in pictures 1 and 2, and elsewhere, were all the result of masking out with tape and newspaper. Quarter-inch tape was used to create the lines of the stonework and pediment; newspaper cut-outs to make other shapes and mask out surrounding areas. Spattering is a time-consuming but striking finish if carried out with a degree of restraint. It can be messy, so it is essential to protect surroundings before you begin. The best tool is a stencil brush, with stiff squared bristles, but here toothbrushes and perfume atomizers have also produced interesting effects. A cheap alternative is a coarse paintbrush with its bristles cut off to make a squared end. After you have decided on a background, experiment with different colours and consistencies – for spattering, paint must be liquid enough to flick easily but thick enough to adhere well to the surface.

Practise different techniques to see which creates the effect you want. You can draw your fingers, or a comb, across the wet bristles or tap the brush against a wooden stick; a perfume atomizer will make a really fine spray. Build colours up gradually and keep the spattering fairly sparse – it's an effect that can easily be overdone. If you use more than one colour, let the paint dry before the next coat.

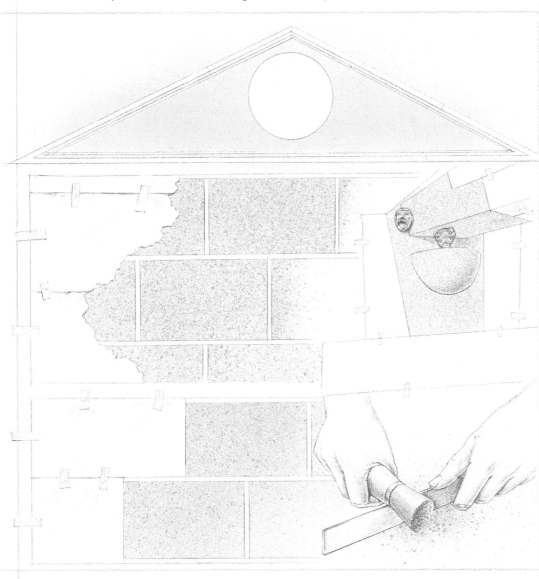

On the coffee table seen in picture 1, several coats of cream emulsion formed the base onto which a slip-coat called 'crackle glaze' was put. Then turquoise oil-based paint was flicked over the top. The whole surface was then covered with a black oil-based glaze. Quick-drying with a hairdryer caused this top coat to pull apart, creating the crazed effect. The same colours in a different sequence were used on the dining table.

The mirror frame and fireplace seen in picture 2 were decorated to blend in with the walls, using various combinations of cream, turquoise, black and brown. For the mirror, a cheap frame was spattered by flicking paint off a toothbrush. Spattering is an adaptable technique and can be used on plasterwork, woodwork, or furniture, provided the surface has been properly prepared, as well as the walls.

5

6

5 The entrance hall skylight runs the full length of the corridor, creating a top-lit gallery for a collection of architectural photographs. In keeping with the formal colour scheme, silk cords suspend the pictures from a traditional picture rail, painted black to match the frames. The photographs themselves were taken by Cathy using a large-format camera which is specially designed for accurate reproduction of architectural detail. Like the gargoyles in the living room, a painted plaster reproduction of an angel carving provides an unusual decorative detail. In another neat touch, the heavy panelled main door is painted black on the outside but cream on the reverse. The matt black door fittings are of Italian design and were relatively expensive compared with standard fittings.

6 The bathroom tiles were applied in a diagonal drawn up by Paul on graph paper – another very simple but striking idea which transforms a standard grid into an interesting decorative detail. This idea works particularly well in a monochrome room – a novel approach that only demanded some skill in tile cutting.

PIONEERING SPIRIT

When businesses decline or move out of the city, they can leave behind acres of still-usable space, sometimes in a prime location. The conversion of light industrial and commercial properties into studios and apartments has been most dramatic in New York, where demand has always been great for accommodation. Originating in SoHo in the early 1970s, with artists setting up studios in disused warehouses, the 'loft' movement quickly reclaimed other derelict districts, introducing New Yorkers to a whole new way of living.

When Melanie and Roger Franklin moved into their loft they were the first residents in the area – at night the only lights came from their building. Roger had lived in two other lofts and found the old printing works through a photographer friend who was looking for a studio. Melanie was impressed by the sweep of space and the building's character. Neither was worried by crossing the frontier from residential streets into an area with few amenities.

The loft itself was in such bad condition that it took a crew of people two weeks just to clear out all the rubbish. Dirt was several inches deep, the walls were black, and steel plates covered parts of the floor where heavy machinery once stood. To assess what was there, Roger had everything painted white; the windows were covered and an electric spray gun was used to speed up the process. Although battered and stained, the wooden floor was kept for its warmth and character. Window frames were stripped down to the original oak and oiled; utility details were deliberately left exposed.

With the basic shell complete, the challenge remained to turn the expanse of space into a home, a task that fell to Melanie. Cleverly designed partition walls make an enclosed area at one end for bedrooms and bathrooms, while in the main space skilful arrangement of furniture has created a series of open 'sitting rooms', each with its own mood. The decor throughout is defined by the colours and patterns displayed in Roger's collection of kelims.

In the last few years, others have followed the Franklins' example and converted commercial buildings nearby. What was once an abandoned and run-down area is gradually being reabsorbed into the mainstream of New York.

1 A formal seating area under the windows is one of three different 'sitting rooms' within the main loft space. Design inspiration has come from a collection of kelim rugs, whose warm earth colours and geometric patterns have been picked up in the choice of furniture. Here the strawberry red of the Japanese chairs makes a vivid contrast with the taupe upholstery of the sofas.

2

2 The dining area features a fine Regency table surrounded by Prague chairs and an Austrian carved walnut armoire on loan from a friend. The large canvas on the wall is by an artist friend, Jeffrey Lew, and measures 2.4m × 1.8m (8ft × 6ft). The 2.4m- (8ft-) high partition wall is the standard height of a sheet of plasterboard or sheetrock and allows light through to the bedrooms.

Large open-plan areas pose special decorating and furnishing problems. While the sheer volume of space is dramatic and exciting, without careful organization the overall effect can end up being simply intimidating. Furniture needs to be large enough to make an impact. Similarly, any pictures must also be selected for size and visibility – a delicate watercolour, for example, would simply disappear against an expanse of wall.

Arranging separate 'rooms' within the space can also help adjust the scale without breaking up the vista. Here even the positioning of the scatter rugs has been carefully considered to direct the flow from area to area.

3

3 The main view down the loft shows the dining area (see 2), a built-in seating area (see 5) and, under the windows, a more formal arrangement (see 1).

Centralized tracks co-ordinate lighting, with spots for accenting details and floodlights for general illumination. Since there is no air conditioning, fans have been installed, their utility design in keeping with the other industrial features.

4 The library corner, to the right of the main area, is furnished with family mementoes and antiques, creating an intimate atmosphere reminiscent of a gentlemen's club. Books line an alcove on open shelves made of stained birch.

5 A built-in banquette makes a contemporary seating area. This was specially constructed using gypsum board for the base, topped with formica for a crisp, durable edge. The sofas are bed-sized cushions covered with forest green corduroy. The glass-topped coffee table allows the kelim to remain in view.

PARIS ROOFTOP

Unlike London, with its streets of terraced houses and residential squares right in the centre of town, Paris is a city of apartment-dwellers. Strict zoning regulations have preserved the unique character of the *quartiers*, much to the benefit of the urban environment as a whole. But this has meant that in the average Parisian home space is a real luxury. This compact but well-planned apartment, constructed in the 1960s on top of an old building in one of Paris's most respectable districts, is a neat, modern solution to the problem of family accommodation in the city.

The apartment, which incorporates a mezzanine floor, pokes up one storey above the mainly six-storey buildings around it. Full advantage has been taken of its location. On the north-facing wall two large windows fit around the slope of the mansard roof, flooding the living area with natural light; the south-facing wall opens out onto a terrace with a splendid view of the Eiffel Tower. Recently, new lighting has been installed all the way up the Tower, meaning that even on cloudy nights the apartment is as bright as if there were a full moon.

Valérie and Marc Duval were already living in the area when they noticed the property advertised in the paper. The quality of the space led to an instant decision and also meant that little had to be done except basic redecoration. The carpet throughout the living area was taken up to expose a parquet floor and the walls and ceilings were repainted in different textures of white and beige to maximize the light. One small room, a closed-off end of the terrace originally used for storing odds and ends, was converted to make a nursery for their new baby. Valérie, who works in the draughting department of an interior design firm, has furnished the apartment with modern pieces sympathetic to the overall design.

Despite the feeling of space generated by the large windows and panoramic views, the total floor area of the apartment is only 100 square metres (1076 sq ft) – no more than a small townhouse. Although space remains a problem, well-organized storage and restrained decor has made the most of the available area. In this apartment good design speaks for itself.

1, 2 The main living area, showing the mezzanine, which is used as a guest bedroom. The large north-facing windows are left uncovered – there is no problem of overlooking neighbours. At the opposite end of the space is a terrace with a panoramic view of Paris.

The apartment only needed basic redecoration. The walls were painted matt white, but

2

gloss was used underneath the mezzanine to create a reflective surface that makes the most of the light. The ceiling is a mid-sheen neutral beige, preventing the room from looking too chilly and drawing in the height a little. The original carpet was taken up to reveal a parquet floor, which was then renovated. The warm tones of polished wood complement the clean modern lines of the structure and furnishing.

3

3 The main bedroom opens off the living area, reached via a door to the left under the mezzanine (see 1). The co-ordination appears effortless. A vivid plaid bedcover dominates the room, its grid of strong colours forming the basis of the contemporary, graphic look. The pair of folding stools at the end of the bed are matched by folding bedside tables – simple furniture that does not overwhelm.

4 The little nursery was the only room that required conversion. Originally just a closed-off end of the terrace, it was basically a shed used for storing junk. The low slanted ceiling (the room is only 2.2 metres [7ft] high) made the space seem even more confined. To make the room appear inviting without drawing it in any further, the walls were painted white and then covered with slatted timber blinds glued in place. A

laminated countertop with built-in storage running the length of one wall makes a practical surface for changing and dressing the baby.

5 The living room is furnished with well-chosen modern pieces that complement the contemporary design of the apartment. An extensive cupboard space under the mezzanine level itself means that the main area is not cluttered up with the family's

possessions, and the furniture can be arranged for maximum impact. The only strong colour in the room is provided by the red leather armchair. The table beside it is one of a pair, a granite-topped steel design reminiscent of Mondrian by Jean Michel Wilmotte, an up-and-coming interior designer. In this resolutely modern setting, the only 'period' pieces are the framed prints showing details of the Opéra and the Place Vendôme.

4

5

HIGH CONTRAST

The bold juxtaposition of modern elegance and decaying surfaces makes this apartment an amusing exercise in contrasts. The contrast is carried right through in colour and texture, with sleek black and chrome set against a warm, sandy background designed to look like old stone.

Skilful application of a variety of special paint techniques has avoided the crisp look that normally accompanies redecoration. The living room walls and ceiling were ragged in several neutral tones to give the impression that they have mellowed with time. All of the details – dados, architraves, door, cornice and picture rails – were painted black and then softened with marbling. In the kitchen, however, the treatment is more tongue-in-cheek. Spidery lines painted on top of a textured finish suggest the cracks of decay. And, running diagonally down the chimney breast, a ragged fissure has been chiselled right through the plasterwork into the brick – the ultimate in distressing.

Against these 'aged' surfaces are set the clean lines of Art Deco. Most of the furniture dates from the 1930s, part of a collection of pieces built up over the years by Roger Britnell, the owner and designer of the apartment. He selected only those items that fit into the monochrome scheme or could be customized to do so – the rest was left in storage.

With inexpensive finishes and little required in the way of new furniture, a relatively high proportion of the budget could be spent on quality details. Roger finally tracked down the chrome electrical sockets and door furniture in Italy. Although they cost much more than standard fittings, they play an important part in maintaining the consistency of the design. Fortunately, the mixer taps in the bathroom were more economically acquired from a brass merchant and then electroplated with chrome. And while the matt black fine blinds were fairly expensive, in the bathroom stick-on leading applied to sandblasted glass made a cheap and instant Gothic window.

Despite the extensive use of black, the apartment manages to feel light and spacious. The pale earth colours of the walls and ceiling are echoed by the wood block kitchen floor and the light cream carpet elsewhere, modifying the severe graphic lines of woodwork and cornice.

1 In the kitchen an L-shaped
layout separates the dining
area from food preparation.
Since this room is often used
for entertaining, the design is
more formal than that of most
kitchens. Wall units, stacked
for maximum storage,
accommodate appliances and
kitchen equipment. To 'age'
the walls, a mixture of
emulsion, filler and fine sand
was spread over the surface.

2 In the dining area, an
inexpensive display cabinet
was made by fitting glass doors
to a bookcase. Stick-on leading
applied to the glass adds
decoration, with a strip of
beading fixed to the top
providing the finishing touch.
   Beneath this cabinet, a
sideboard houses the washing
machine.
   On top of the sandy textured
finish, cracks were painted in
freehand, using artists' stains.

125

The glass shelves which carry stereo equipment are neatly bracketed with solid metal screw-in door bolts, available at specialist stores which sell door furniture. They are strong and eliminate the need for unsightly, bulky fittings.

3 In one corner of the living room a neat recess has been made to house the stereo system. Trimmed with strips of wooden moulding and painted with matt black eggshell, it is fitted with unobtrusive glass shelves to carry the record deck, tape recorder and amplifier – equipment often at odds with the style of an interior. The chrome-faced speaker does look at home on the Savoy trolley, a 1930s' design.

4 Above the kitchen fireplace, a jagged crack turns a traditional focal point into a talking point. A daring gesture, it was created by chiselling through the plasterwork of the chimney breast right into the brick wall. Matt polyurethane varnish was then applied to prevent the surface from disintegrating any further. The fireplace itself is an addition – the original had been removed and the hearth bricked up. It is painted matt black.

5 An Art Deco light and chrome figure shines out against the black marbled dado. To make the dado, tongue-and-groove panels were applied around all four walls of the living room. On top of a base coat of matt black eggshell, lines of white and grey oil-based paint were diffused to create a stylized form of marbling. The finish looked a little glossy at first, so matt varnish was used to tone it down.

When you redesign your home or move to a new place, the furniture that you have collected over the years may not work together in the new interior. The answer is to be selective – store or get rid of those pieces that don't fit in, and adapt others if possible.

7

6 The living room, originally divided into two, provides a spacious area for entertaining. Instead of being arranged in conventional seating patterns, furniture is set back against the walls to increase the floor area. Like the stereo system, the television is set into a recess, which was once a fireplace. The black bands of the ceiling moulding and picture rail link the space together. Like the dado, these were additions, painted black

and then marbled to soften their impact. Matt black fine blinds also give graphic interest. To offset the severity of the detailing, the walls were ragged in shades of ochre and beige emulsion, with cream used as a highlight. Similar shades, with the addition of grey, were ragged on the ceiling, using a crisper cloth for a bolder print. All the colours, the result of extensive experimentation, were mixed using artists' stains.

7 In the bathroom, sandblasted glass was installed in the window to retain privacy without sacrificing any light. Stick-on leading creates the effect of Gothic tracery cheaply and instantly. Pursuing the same theme, three wooden panels, originally sections from church pews, make a richly detailed frame over a sheet of mirrors. Tongue-and-groove panels were applied around the walls. Like the window frame, these

were stained to a dark mahogany colour and then sealed with matt polyurethane varnish.

The old-fashioned claw-foot enamel bathtub was acquired secondhand and fitted with period taps. Reproductions are now made of such designs but they are very expensive. These taps were discovered at a brass merchant's, restored and then electroplated for a fraction of the cost.

INDEX AND ACKNOWLEDGMENTS

Art of Living (pp.32–7): John Pawson (architect)
Back to School (pp.26–31): Graham Carr (interior designer and paint effects)
Disappearing Trick (pp.54–9): Don Kaufman (colourist)
Empire Line (pp.94–9): Ed Carroll (architect and designer)
High Contrast (pp.124–7): Giuseppina de Camillo (drawings and murals); R.W. Phillips (murals); John Ebdon (paint effects)
Illusions of Grandeur (pp.110–15): Simons Design Consultants; Nick Welsh and Claire Maclean (specialist decorators); P.R. Hodgkinson (furniture design)
Lateral Thinking (pp.82–5): Horne Architects
Past Revisited (pp.86–93): Mary Lou Arscott (architect)
Period Features (pp.10–15): Jerry Hewitt (architect); Angela Hewitt-Woods (interior decorator and soft furnishings)
Self-Assembly (pp 64–7): Pedro Guedes of Berman and Guedes Architects (design and assembly)
Ship-Shape (pp.76–81): Robert T. Bayley (architect)

Split Level (pp.22–5) Carl Falck (architect); Robert Alder (kitchen design); Simon Brady (paint finishes)

The publishers and authors would like to thank the following for their kind assistance:
Vivienne Bateson, Pierette Pompon Bailhache, Gille Bouchez, Karen Bowen, Catherine Carpenter, Walter Chatham, Bénédicte Cartigny, Fiona Dunlop, Hilary French, June Goldberg, Nicolas Goldsmith, John Hurley, Martin Lazenby *(for architectural advice)*, Maggie Malone, Robert Marino, Edward Marshner, Sarah Miller, Randy Ostrow, Bobby Queen, Suzanne Slesin, Charlotte Smith and Polly Wreford.